W9-API-134

Adult Piano Method

Lessons, Solos, Technique & Theory

Fred Kern · Phillip Keveren · Barbara Kreader · Mona Rejino

Welcome to the piano! Whether you are a beginner or a student returning to the piano after a break in your study, the music in the **Hal Leonard Adult Piano Method** will excite your interest and imagination. You will find:

- Classical, folk, pop, rock and jazz music with adult appeal
- Realistic pacing that challenges without overwhelming

In addition, you will find:

- **Music Theory** that relates to the music you are playing
- **Technique Tips** that teach you how your physical motions relate to the sounds you want to make
- **Style Clips** that help you with musical interpretation
- **Ad Libs** that teach you how to improvise
- **Quick-Licks** that introduce you to familiar musical clichés so you can sound like a pro right away

Best of all, each book comes with a CD or GM disk, allowing you to play along with an orchestral accompaniment for each piece! Using this model for a polished performance, you will find yourself playing with:

- Increased rhythmic security
- Musical feeling
- Appropriate style

May the **Hal Leonard Adult Piano Method** guide you as you accomplish your life-long goal of learning to play the piano, bringing more music to your life!

Best wishes,

Fred Kern   *Phillip Keveren*   *Barbara Kreader*   *Mona Rejino*

Edited by Alice Brovan

Book/CD: ISBN 0-634-06626-9
Book/GM: ISBN 0-634-06628-5

HAL•LEONARD®
CORPORATION

7777 W. BLUEMOUND RD. P.O. BOX 13819 MILWAUKEE, WI 53213

In Australia Contact:
Hal Leonard Australia Pty. Ltd.
4 Lentara Court
Cheltenham, Victoria, 3192 Australia
Email: ausadmin@halleonard.com

Visit Hal Leonard Online at
www.halleonard.com

CONTENTS

Full orchestral arrangements, available on CD or GM disk, may be used for both performance and rehearsal:

 The first track number is a practice tempo. The second track number is the performance tempo.

 The GM disk has only one track per title and is a preset performance tempo. GM disk tracks can be slowed down to any practice tempo desired, and can also be made faster than the set tempo at will.

Preparation to Play

Sitting at the Piano

- Sit tall and lean slightly forward, balancing your body weight on the front half of the piano bench.
- Keep your feet flat on the floor.
- Adjust the bench height so that your forearm is parallel to the floor and your fingertips are touching the surface of the keys.

Hand Position

Let your arms hang relaxed at your sides. Notice how your hands stay gently curved.

Keep your hands relaxed and curved as you raise them to the piano keyboard.

When you are playing the piano, keep your fingers in this relaxed, curved position.

Finger Numbers

Place your hands together with fingertips touching.

    Tap fingers 1 (thumbs)
    Tap fingers 2
    Tap fingers 3
    Tap fingers 4
    Tap fingers 5

Tap this finger exercise on the closed lid of the keyboard.

1. **R.H.**   1-1-3-3   1-1-5-5   4-3-2-1   5-5-5-5
2. **L.H.**   5-5-3-3   4-4-1-1   2-3-4-5   1-1-1-5

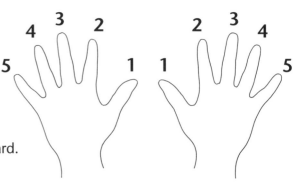

Finger Numbers

Piano Keyboard – Two Black Keys

The black keys are divided into groups of twos and threes.

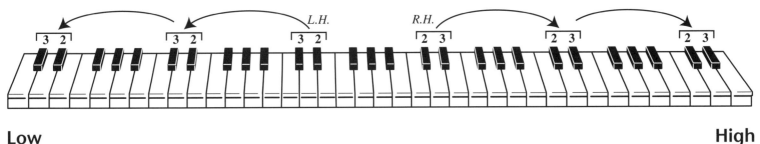

Low   **High**

Using your **left hand**, start in the middle of the keyboard and play the groups of two black keys with fingers 2-3 going **down the keyboard to the left**.

Using your **right hand**, start in the middle of the keyboard and play the groups of two black keys with fingers 2-3 going **up the keyboard to the right**.

| **Technique Tip** | **Beautiful Tone** |

Use weight from your whole arm as you play each key. Let your arm follow your fingers.

| **Ad Lib** | **An Improvisation** |

Improvise your own melody.
With your right and left hands, choose any groups of two black keys in the upper part of the piano. Listen and feel the pulse as your teacher plays the accompaniment below. When you are ready, play along, making up your own melody.

Accompaniment
Swing (♩ = 104)   TRACK 1   TRACK 1

The Beat Goes On

Pulse – The Heartbeat of Music

Like your body's heartbeat, music has a pulse. The beat can move at fast, medium, or slow speeds.

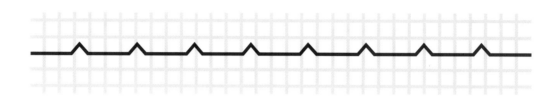

Tap your foot with the beat as your teacher plays the musical examples below at three different speeds.

Three Black Keys

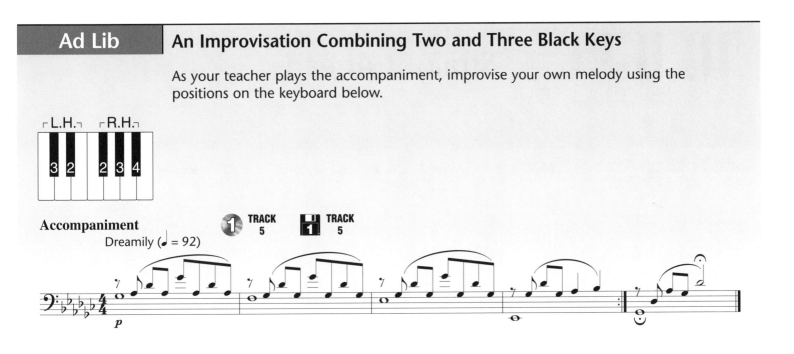

Low   **High**

Using your **left hand**, start in the middle of the keyboard and play the groups of three black keys with fingers 2-3-4 going **down the keyboard**.

Using your **right hand**, start in the middle of the keyboard and play the groups of three black keys with fingers 2-3-4 going **up the keyboard**.

Ad Lib	An Improvisation Combining Two and Three Black Keys

As your teacher plays the accompaniment, improvise your own melody using the positions on the keyboard below.

┌ **L.H.** ┐   ┌ **R.H.** ┐

3 2   2 3 4

Accompaniment
Dreamily (♩ = 92)

TRACK 5   TRACK 5

p

Ad Lib	An Improvisation Using Three Black Keys

Using your right or left hand, choose any group of three black keys in the upper part of the piano. Listen and feel the pulse as your teacher plays the accompaniment below, then improvise your own black-key melody and play along.

Accompaniment
With a bounce (♩ = 120)

TRACK 6   TRACK 6

mf

Technique Tip — Attention to Rests

During each rest, release your arm weight, keeping your fingers on the surface of the keys.

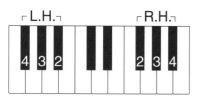

Straight Ahead

Clap the rhythm of this piece before you play it. Play the first line with your right hand, followed by the second line with your left hand.

Steady ($\downarrow$ = 120)

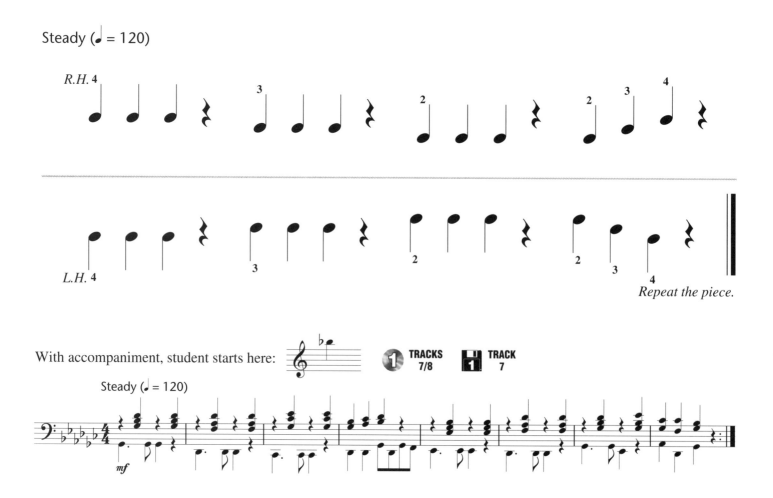

Repeat the piece.

With accompaniment, student starts here:

MEASURES

Bar lines group beats into **Measures**.

HALF NOTE

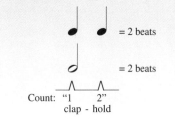

A **Half Note** fills the time of two quarter notes.

= 2 beats

= 2 beats

Count: "1   2"
clap - hold

WHOLE NOTE

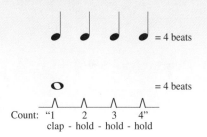

A **Whole Note** fills the time of four quarter notes.

= 4 beats

= 4 beats

Count: "1   2   3   4"
clap - hold - hold - hold

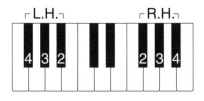

Opening Night

Folk Melody

Upbeat tempo ($\bullet$ = 120)

R.H.

L.H.

Double Bar Line means the end of the piece.

With accompaniment, student starts here:

TRACKS 9/10   **TRACK 8**

Upbeat tempo ($\bullet$ = 120)

mf

9

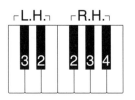

Water Lily

Phillip Keveren

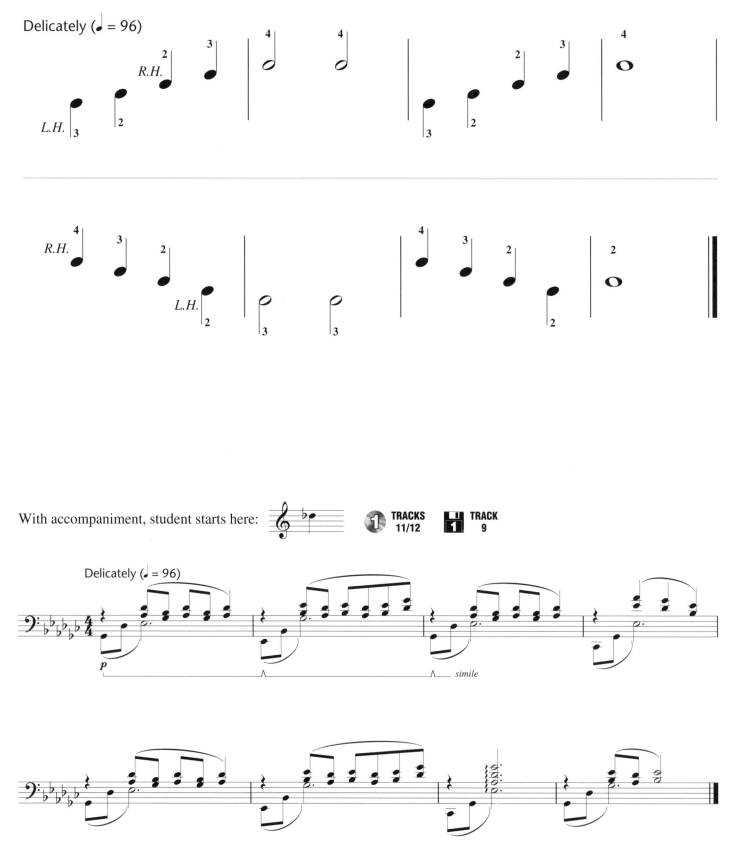

The Music Alphabet
Playing on the White Keys

A-B-C-D-E-F-G

Music uses the first seven letters of the alphabet. These letters are used over and over to name the white keys.

Put your thumb behind the first joint of your third finger. Play and say the music alphabet using this rhythm.

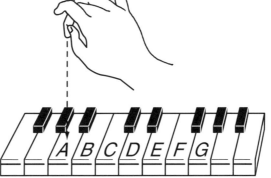

Fred Kern

Floating (♩ = 80)

Play each note with the third finger.

R.H.

With accompaniment, student starts here:

TRACKS 13/14   TRACK 10

C-D-E Groups

Technique Tip | When using your thumb, let it rest naturally on its outside tip.

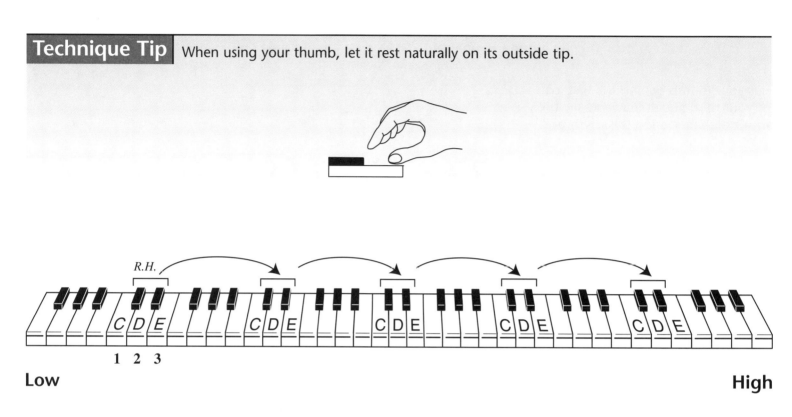

Low   **High**

With your right hand, start at the low end of the keyboard and play the **C-D-E** groups with individual fingers 1-2-3 going up the keyboard.

Now explore the keyboard, playing the **C-D-E** groups with your left hand, using fingers 3-2-1.

Ad Lib | **An Improvisation**

Using your right or left hand, choose any **C-D-E** group in the upper part of the piano. Listen and feel the pulse as your teacher plays the accompaniment below. Join in and play **C-D-E**. Next play **E-D-C** and experiment by mixing the letters in any order to create your own melody.

Accompaniment   **TRACK 15**   **TRACK 11**
Bouncy (♩ = 126)

Playing Forte *f*

Press the key to the bottom of the keybed with full arm weight.

FORTE

f

means play loudly

Party Cat

Phillip Keveren

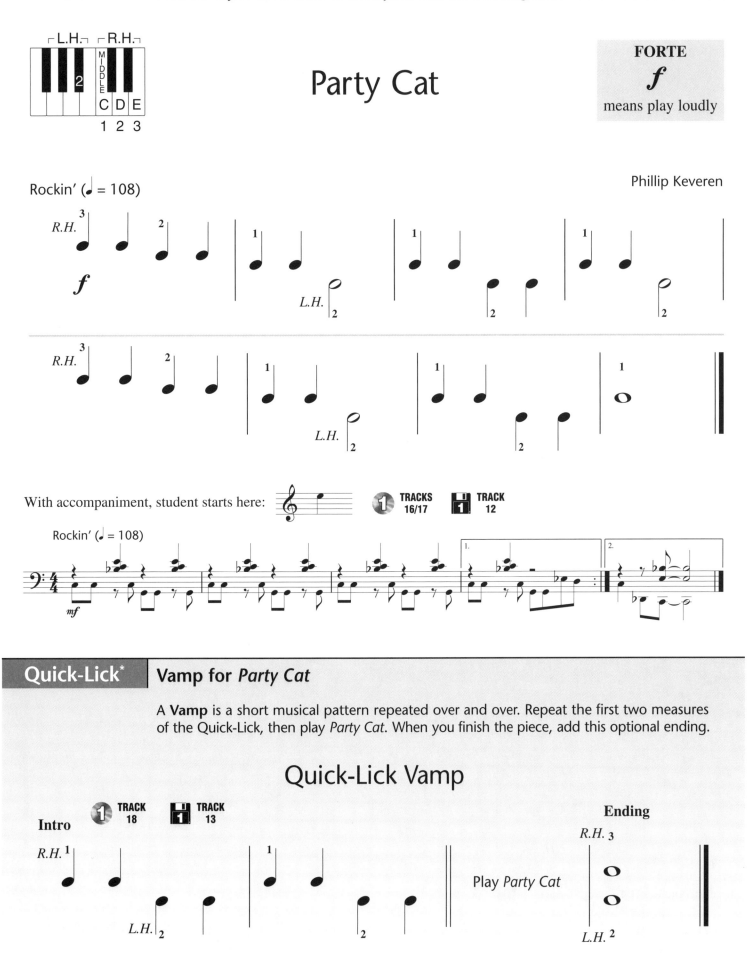

Rockin' (♩ = 108)

With accompaniment, student starts here:

TRACKS 16/17   TRACK 12

Rockin' (♩ = 108)

Quick-Lick* | **Vamp for *Party Cat***

A **Vamp** is a short musical pattern repeated over and over. Repeat the first two measures of the Quick-Lick, then play *Party Cat*. When you finish the piece, add this optional ending.

Quick-Lick Vamp

Intro   TRACK 18   TRACK 13   **Ending**

Play *Party Cat*

*A "lick" is a musical cliché often used in popular music.

Impressionism: *Aloft* is written in an Impressionistic musical style. This music of the late-19th and early-20th centuries originated in France and used melodies and subtle shifts in harmony to hint at, rather than state, mood, place, or natural events. For further enjoyment, listen to recordings of music by the French composers Claude Debussy (*Clair de Lune*) and Maurice Ravel (*Le tombeau de Couperin*).

Listen as your teacher plays the Style Clip below.

Impressionism

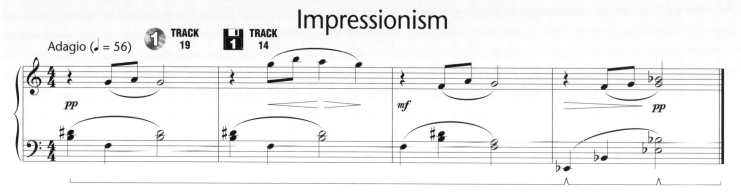

Press the key to the bottom of the keybed with less arm weight.

Aloft

PIANO
p
means play softly

Phillip Keveren

Soaring (♩ = 104)
Hold down the right pedal (damper pedal) throughout.

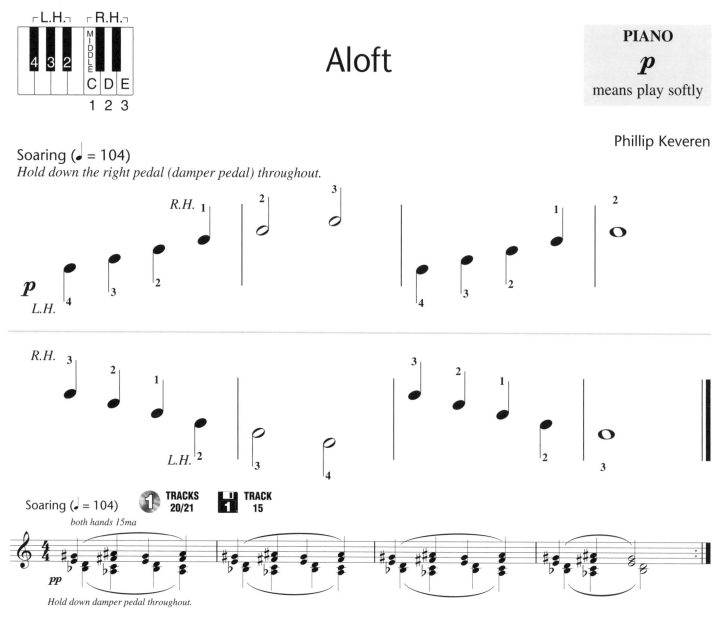

Soaring (♩ = 104)

both hands 15ma

Hold down damper pedal throughout.

14

F-G-A-B Groups

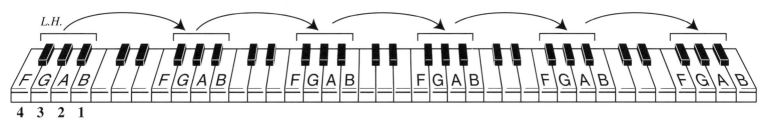

Low   **High**

With your left hand, start at the low end of the keyboard and play the **F-G-A-B** groups with individual fingers 4-3-2-1 going up the keyboard.

Now explore the keyboard, playing the **F-G-A-B** groups with your right hand, using fingers 1-2-3-4.

| **Ad Lib** | **An Improvisation Using F-G-A-B** |

Using your left or right hand, choose any **F-G-A-B** group in the upper part of the piano. Listen and feel the pulse as your teacher plays the accompaniment below. Join in and play **F-G-A-B**, then experiment by mixing the letters in any pattern to improvise your own melody.

Accompaniment
Rock beat (♩ = 126)

TRACK 22   TRACK 16

| **Ad Lib** | **An Improvisation Using F-G-A-B and Two Black Keys** |

Using the positions below, make up your own melody as you play along with the teacher accompaniment.

Accompaniment
Gently (♩ = 88)

TRACK 23   TRACK 17

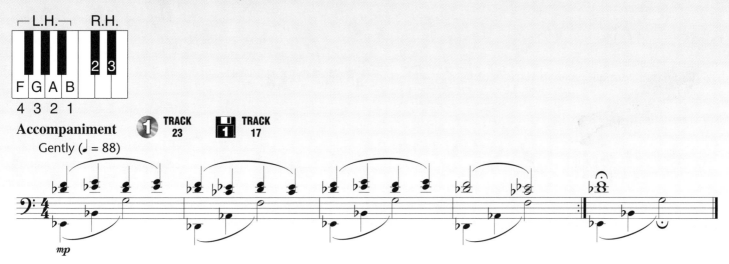

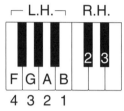

Traffic Jam

Phillip Keveren

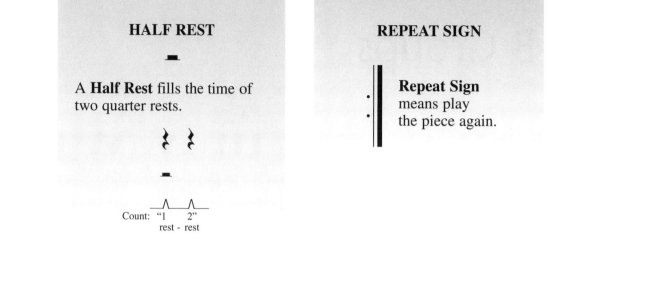

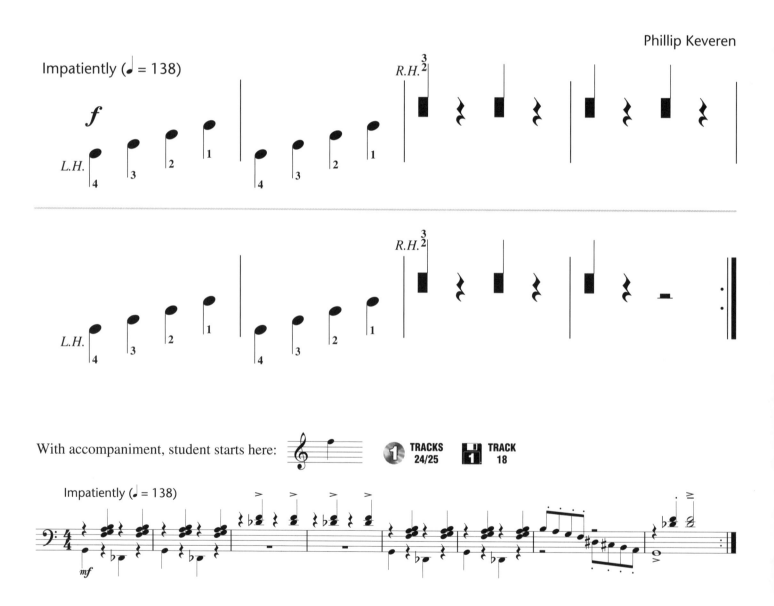

With accompaniment, student starts here:

TRACKS 24/25   TRACK 18

Music Reading

1. Notes move in only three ways: higher, lower, or repeated (staying the same).

   Step   Movement from one key to the very next key (up or down).

   Skip   Movement that begins on one key, skips a key, and plays the next key (up or down).

   Repeat   Movement that continues on the same key (neither higher nor lower).

2. Rhythm in reading involves pulse, time, and note values such as quarter notes, half notes, and whole notes.

Ear Training

1. Your teacher will play each of the four musical examples in any order. Listen carefully to the rhythm of the notes and observe the steps, skips, or repeats.

2. Write the numbers of the examples in the order in which they are played.

   _____   _____   _____   _____

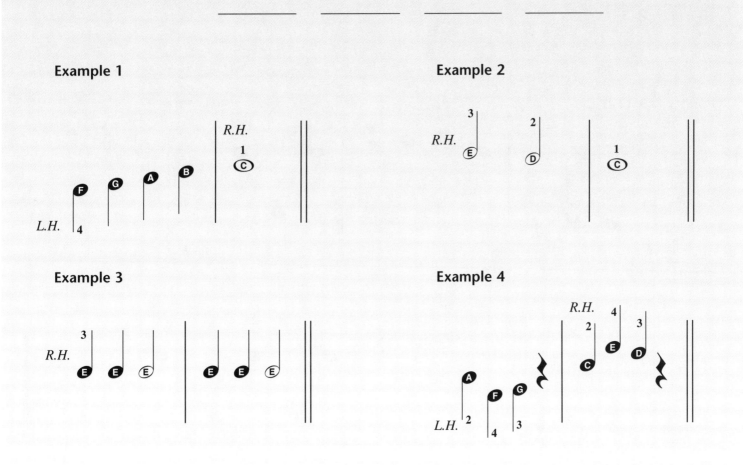

Example 1

Example 2

Example 3

Example 4

Reading

1. Read and play each example above.

2. Experiment by playing the examples in different orders. To create your own piece, choose the order that sounds best to you.

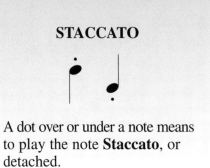

STACCATO

A dot over or under a note means to play the note **Staccato**, or detached.

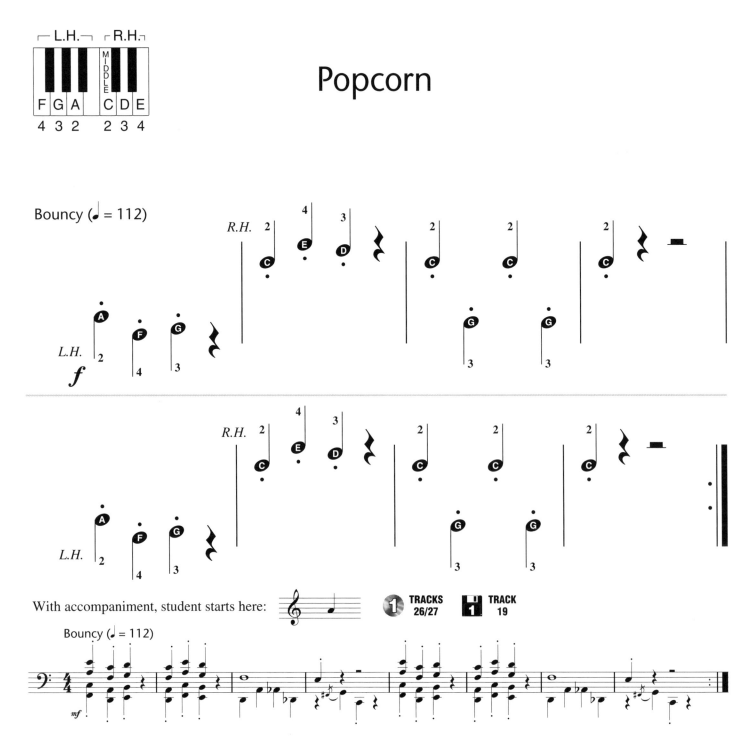

Technique Tip | **Playing Staccato**

To play *staccato*, release the key as soon as you play it, letting your wrist bounce lightly. Notice how your finger naturally rebounds and comes to rest on the key.

Popcorn

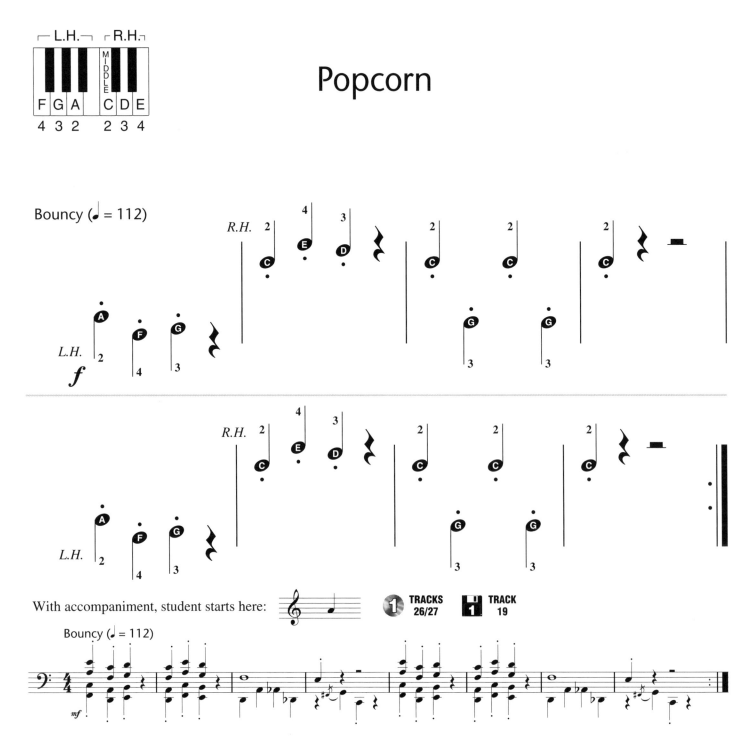

With accompaniment, student starts here:

TRACKS 26/27   **TRACK 19**

LEGATO

Legato indicates smooth and connected playing with no break in the sound.

SLUR

Slur means to play *legato* and is indicated by a curved line over or under several notes.

PHRASE

A **Phrase** is a musical clause or sentence. Slurs often divide the music into phrases.

Technique Tip | **Playing Legato**

To play *legato*, pass the sound smoothly from one finger to the next.

Star to Star

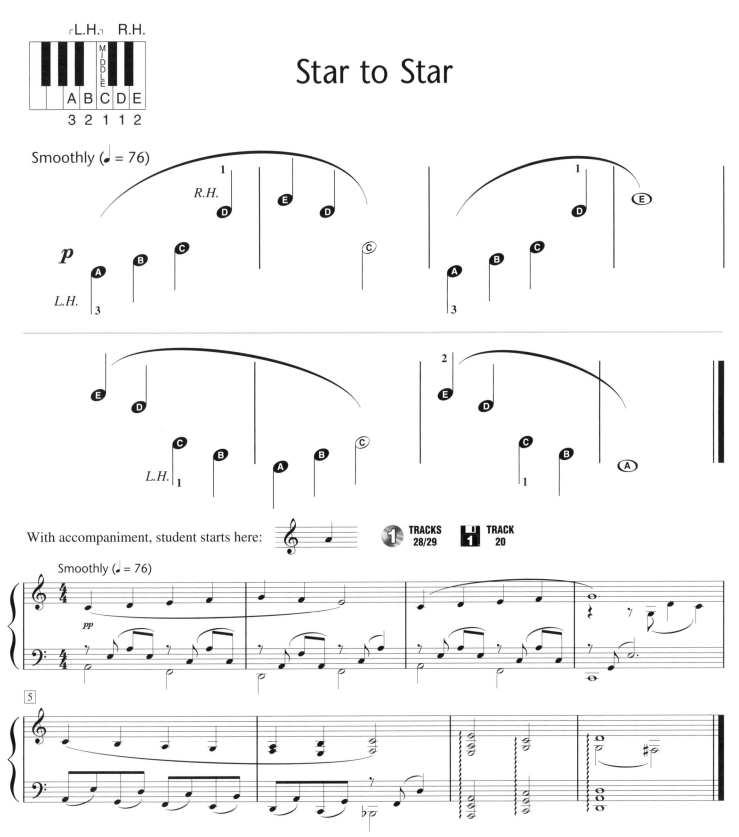

With accompaniment, student starts here:

TRACKS 28/29   TRACK 20

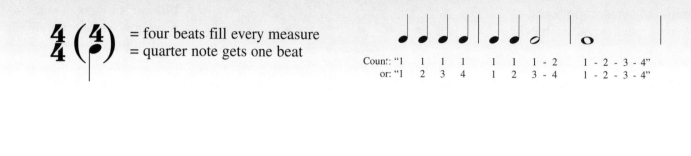

$\frac{4}{4}$ TIME SIGNATURE

$\frac{4}{4}$ = four beats fill every measure
= quarter note gets one beat

Count: "1   1   1   1   1   1   1 - 2   1 - 2 - 3 - 4"
or: "1   2   3   4   1   2   3 - 4   1 - 2 - 3 - 4"

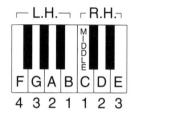

Bermuda Bound

Fred Kern

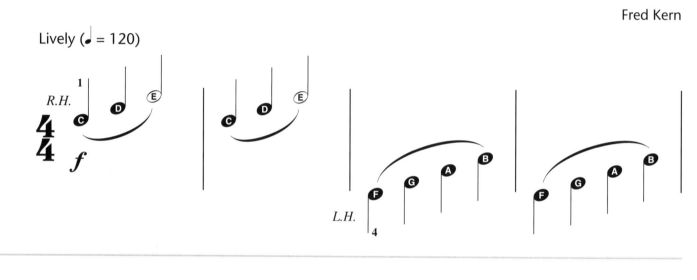

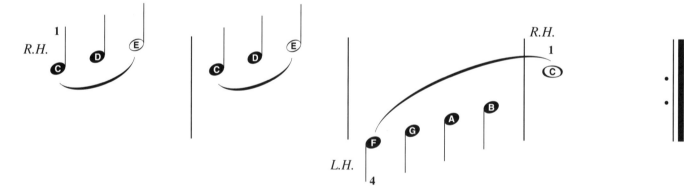

With accompaniment, student starts here:

TRACKS 30/31   TRACK 21

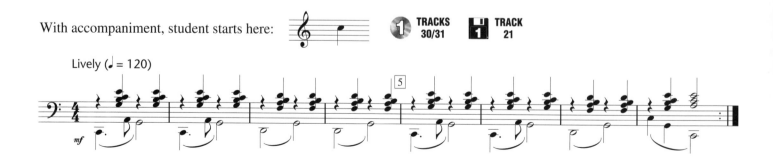

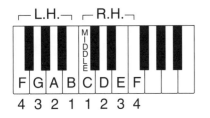

Star Quest

Phillip Keveren

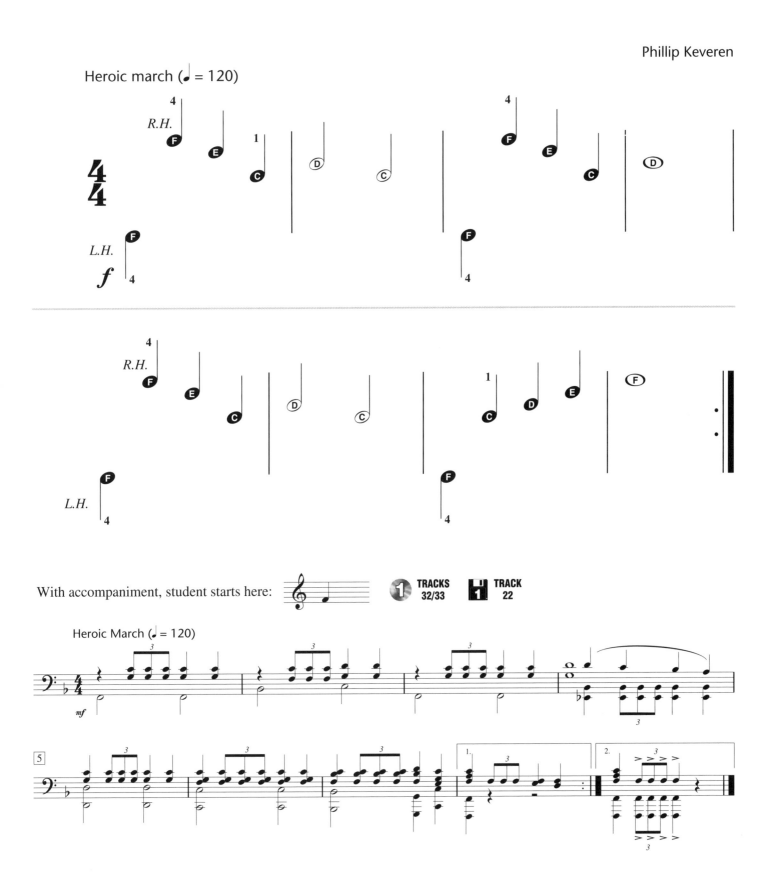

By the River's Edge

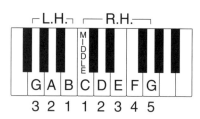

Carol Klose

Quietly flowing along (♩ = 120)

Play legato throughout. When playing without accompaniment, this piece may be played with damper pedal held down throughout.

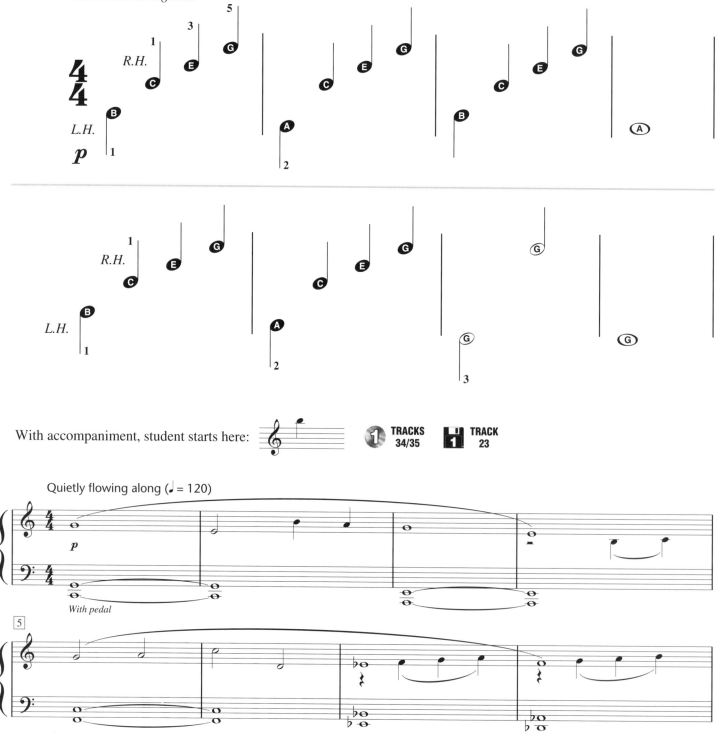

With accompaniment, student starts here:

TRACKS 34/35   TRACK 23

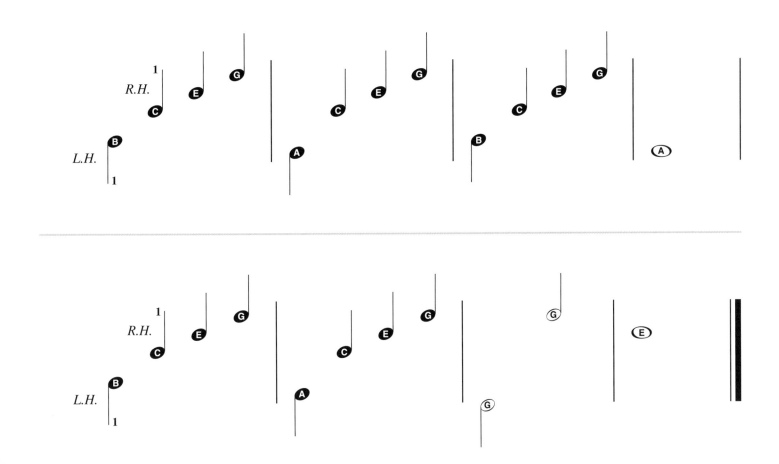

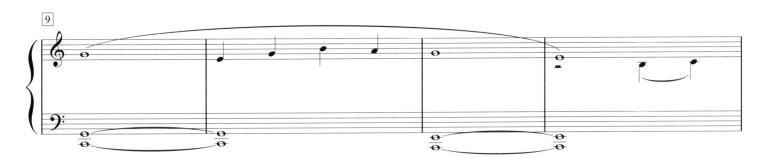

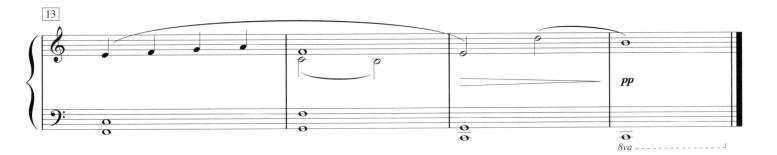

Lines and Spaces

Notes are written on **lines** and in **spaces**.

Line Note   **Space Note**

Music is written on a STAFF of 5 lines and 4 spaces.

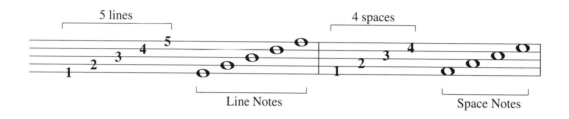

5 lines   4 spaces

Line Notes   Space Notes

Reading Music on the Staff

Repeated Notes   **Steps**

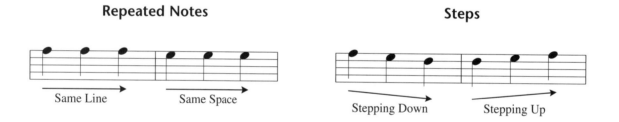

Same Line   Same Space   Stepping Down   Stepping Up

You already know how to play *Straight Ahead*. Now read it on the staff.

⌐L.H.¬

F G A MIDDLE C
4 3 2

Straight Ahead

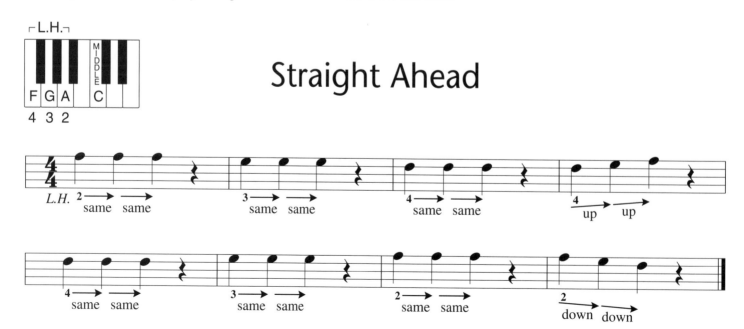

L.H. 2 → →
same same

3 → →
same same

4 → →
same same

4
up   up

4 → →
same same

3 → →
same same

2 → →
same same

2
down down

Reading Notes in the BASS CLEF
(The F Clef)

𝄢

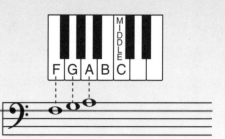

This is the F line

_____

The F line passes between
the two dots of the **Bass Clef** sign.

You will usually play the notes written
on the Bass Staff with your **left hand**.

**The note F is the reading guide
for the Bass Clef.** You can name
any note on the Bass Staff by
moving up or down from the F line.

Laid Back

Reading Notes in the TREBLE CLEF
(The G Clef)

This is the G line

The G line passes through
the curl of the **Treble Clef** sign.

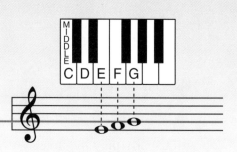

You will usually play the notes written
on the Treble Staff with your **right hand**.

**The note G is the reading guide
for the Treble Clef.** You can name
any note on the Treble Staff by
moving up or down from the G line.

Twilight

Smoothly (= 96)

R.H. 4

p

Accompaniment (Student plays one octave higher than written.) **1** TRACKS 40/41   **TRACK 26**

Smoothly (= 96)

pp

Private Eye

Mysteriously (= 120)

R.H. 4

p

Accompaniment (Student plays one octave higher than written.) **1** TRACKS 42/43   **TRACK 27**

Mysteriously (= 120)

pp

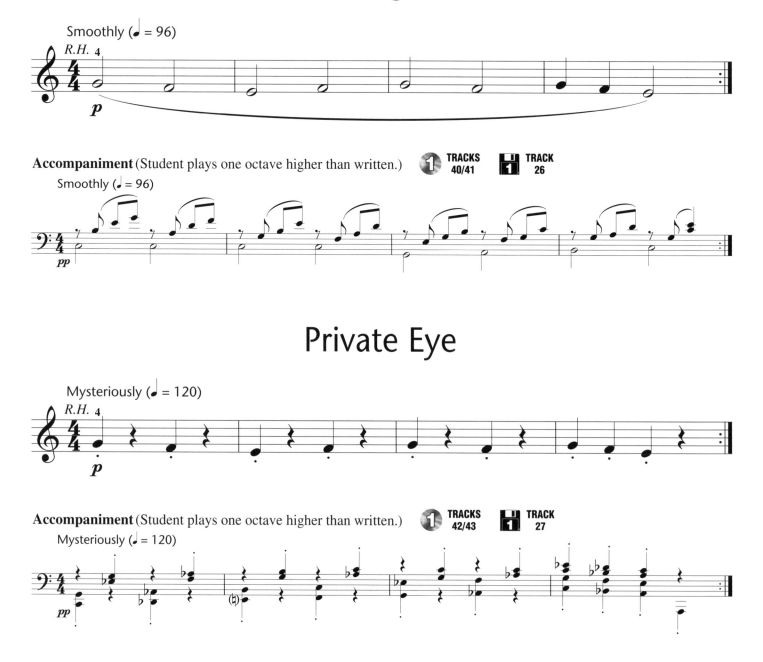

The Grand Staff

The Bass Staff and the Treble Staff together make the **Grand Staff**.

Middle C uses the short line (ledger line) between the Bass Staff and Treble Staff.

Partly Cloudy

Folk Melody

Gently (♩ = 100)

Accompaniment (Student plays one octave higher than written.)

TRACKS 44/45   TRACK 28

Gently (♩ = 100)

When playing a two-note slur, use a drop/lift motion.

Prepare to "shift gears" between **slurs** and **staccatos** by mastering the different motions in each hand.

Clear Skies

Folk Melody

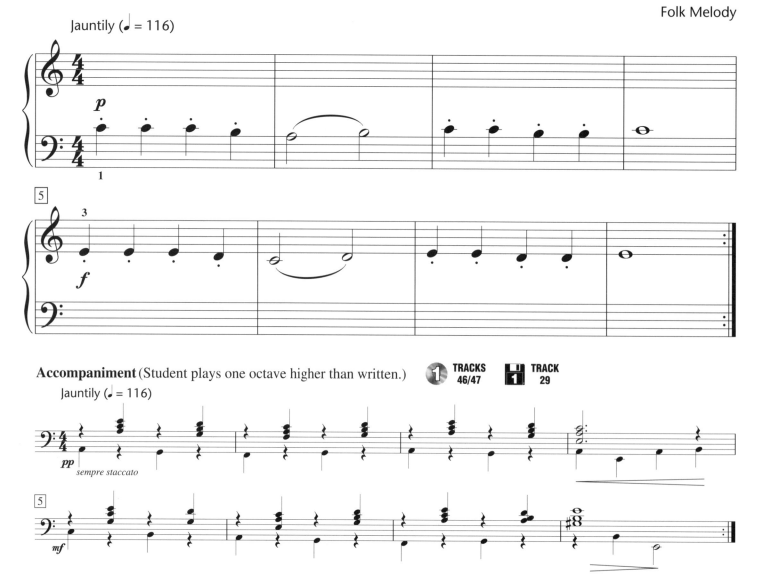

Accompaniment (Student plays one octave higher than written.)

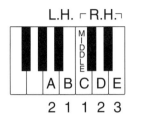

L.H. ┌ R.H. ┐
A B C D E
2 1 1 2 3

Tambourine Tune

Folk Melody

INTERVAL

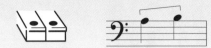

An **Interval** is the distance from one note to another. On the piano, a **2nd** moves from one key to the next. On the staff, a **2nd** moves from a line to a space or a space to a line.

Accompaniment (Student plays one octave higher than written.)

TRACKS 48/49   TRACK 30

With spirit (♩ = 152)

pp - mf

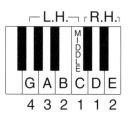

MEZZO PIANO

mp

means medium soft

MEZZO FORTE

mf

means medium loud

Wishful Thinking

Mona Rejino

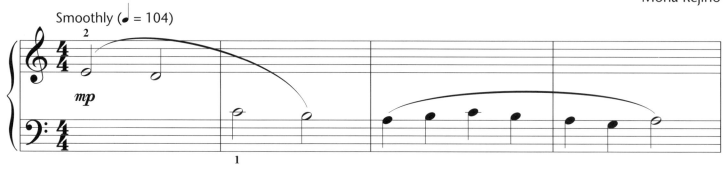

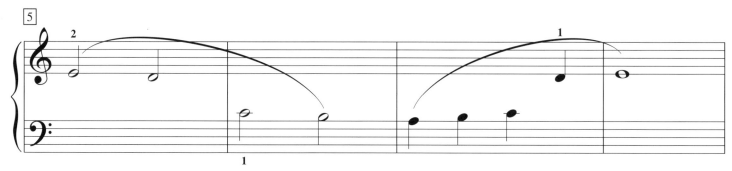

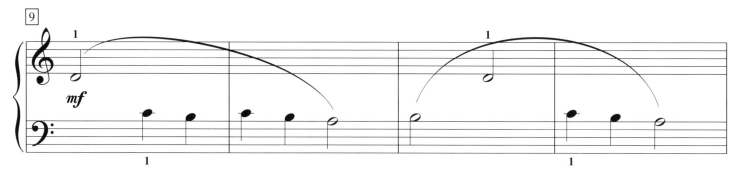

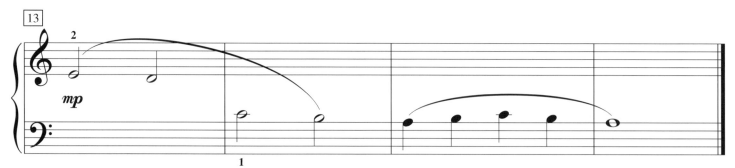

Accompaniment (Student plays one octave higher than written.)

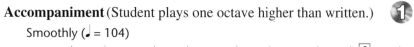

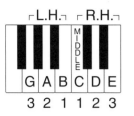

Barefoot on the Beach

Phillip Keveren

| Ad Lib | An Improvisation to *Barefoot on the Beach* |

To improvise a contrasting section to *Barefoot on the Beach*:
- keep your hands in the **A-B-C-D-E** position.
- improvise as your teacher plays the accompaniment below.
- return to the main melody (the "head," in jazz slang).

Accompaniment (Student plays one octave higher than written.)

TRACKS 52/53   TRACK 32

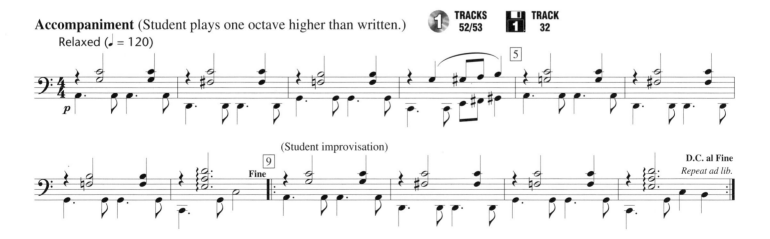

31

Long, Long Ago

Thomas Haynes Bailey

Accompaniment (Student plays two octaves higher than written.)

TRACKS 54/55   TRACK 33

Peacefully (♩ = 120)

With pedal

SKIPS
(3rds)

Line to Line

Skip up
(3rd)

On the piano, a 3rd
– skips a key
– skips a finger
– skips a letter

Space to Space

Skip down
(3rd)

On the staff, a 3rd skips
a letter from either
– line to line or
– space to space

Surprise Symphony

Joseph Haydn
(1732–1809)

Lively (♩ = 132)

TRACKS 56/57   TRACK 34

mf

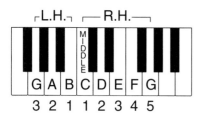

Let Me Fly!

Spiritual
Arranged by Fred Kern

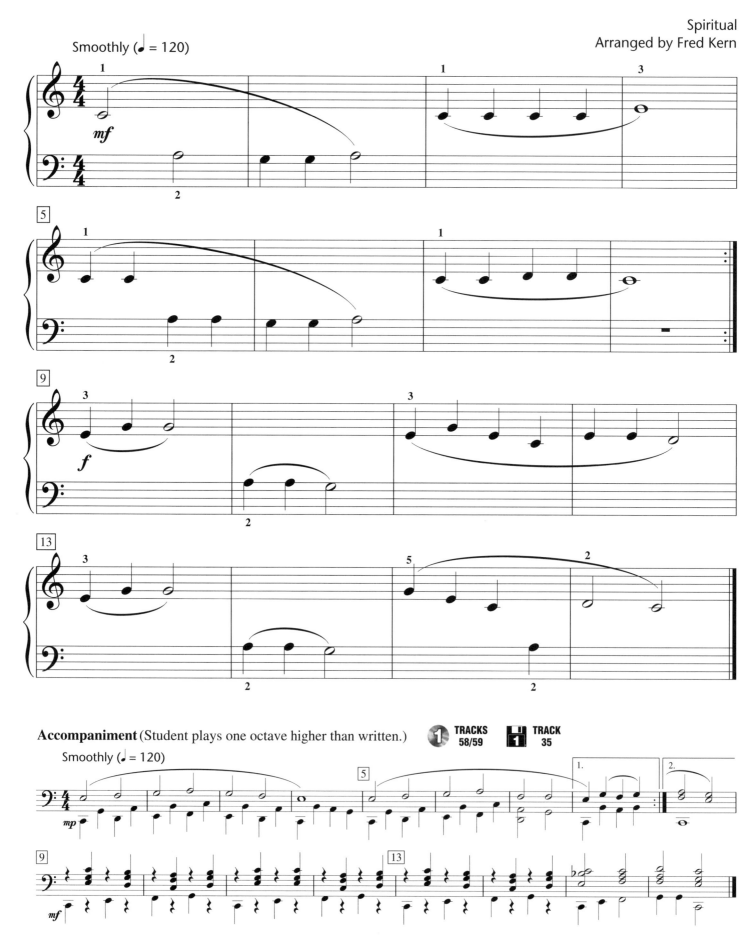

Accompaniment (Student plays one octave higher than written.)

TRACKS 58/59   TRACK 35

Smoothly (♩ = 120)

Reading Intervals

1. **Step**   Notes that move from a line to the very next space, or from a space to the very next line, up or down
2. **Skip**   Notes that move from line-to-line or space-to-space, up or down
3. **Repeat**   Notes that stay on the same line or space

Look carefully at the excerpts below. Observe how the notes move by **Step**, **Skip**, or **Repeat**. Circle the appropriate description below each example, then play the excerpts on the piano.

1. Long, Long Ago

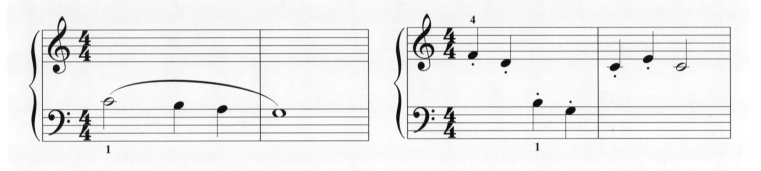

Step, Skip, or Repeat

2. Surprise Symphony

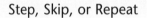

Step, Skip, or Repeat

3. Let Me Fly

Step, Skip, or Repeat

4. Wishful Thinking

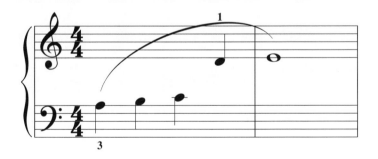
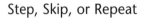

Step, Skip, or Repeat

The Wild Rest

Bill Boyd

Accompaniment (Student plays one octave higher than written.)

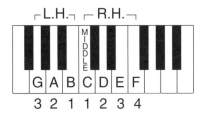

Happy Heart

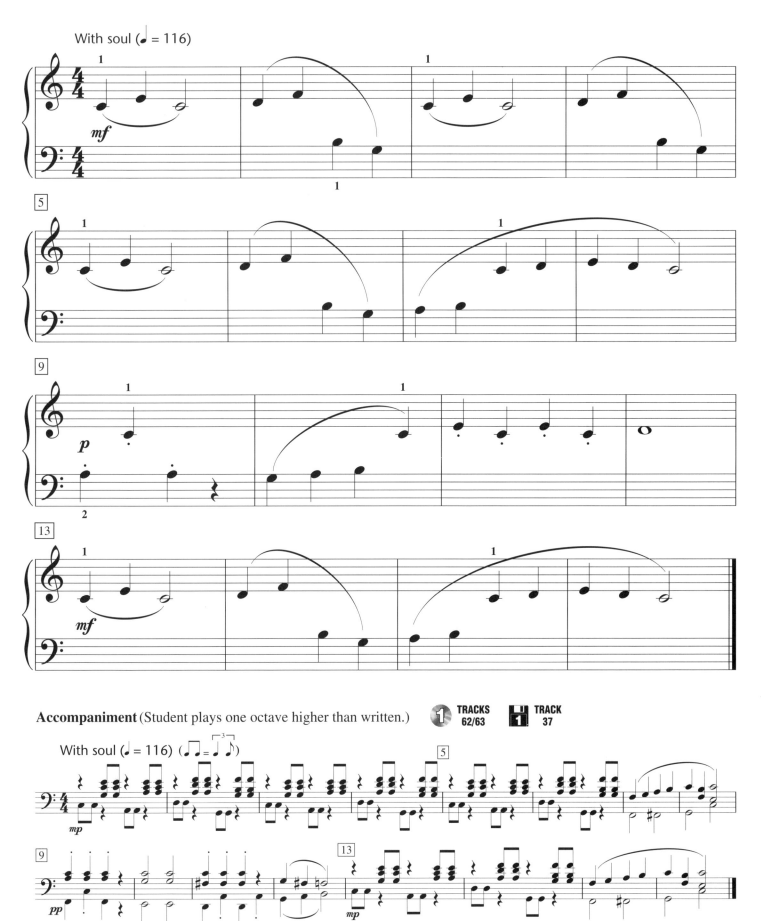

Accompaniment (Student plays one octave higher than written.)

TRACKS 62/63   TRACK 37

DOTTED HALF NOTE

A **Dotted Half Note** fills the time of three quarter notes.

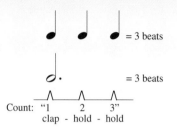

= 3 beats

= 3 beats

Count: "1   2   3"
       clap - hold - hold

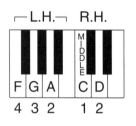

Camptown Races

Stephen Foster
(1826 – 1864)

Lively (♩ = 160)

Accompaniment (Student plays one octave higher than written.)

TRACKS 64/65   TRACK 38

Lively (♩ = 160)

$\frac{3}{4}$ TIME SIGNATURE

$\frac{3}{4}\left(\dfrac{3}{\text{♩}}\right)$ = three beats fill every measure
= quarter note gets one beat

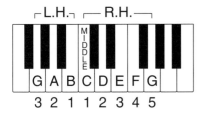

Scottish Air

Folk Melody

Repeat from measure 5.

Accompaniment (Student plays one octave higher than written.)

With spirit (♩ = 144)

TRACKS
66/67

TRACK
39

A Sample of a Musical Style Introducing *The Emperor Waltz*

The waltz originated in Austria in the late 18th century and became popular in Vienna as a flirtatious dance. The prolific waltz composer, Johann Strauss, Jr. (1825-1899), composed over 500 waltzes, taking this dance form to orchestral heights by introducing it into his operettas. For further enjoyment, listen to Viennese waltzes by Johann Strauss, Jr. *(On the Beautiful Blue Danube)* and Franz Lehar *(The Merry Widow Waltz)*.

Listen as your teacher plays the Style Clip below.

Viennese Waltz

Phillip Keveren

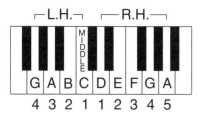

The Emperor Waltz

Johann Strauss, Jr.
(1825-1899)
Arranged by Phillip Keveren

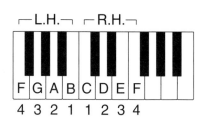

Ocean Breezes

TIE

two notes = one sound

1 - 2 - 3   tie-2 - 3

A **Tie** is a curved line that connects two notes of the same pitch. Hold one sound for the combined value of both notes.

Mona Rejino

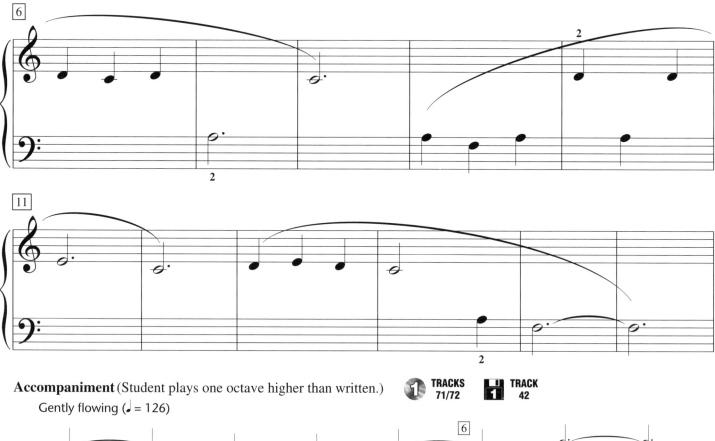

Gently flowing (♩ = 126)
Play both hands one octave higher.

mp

Hold down damper pedal throughout. (Solo)

Accompaniment (Student plays one octave higher than written.)

TRACKS 71/72   TRACK 42

Gently flowing (♩ = 126)

p With pedal

42

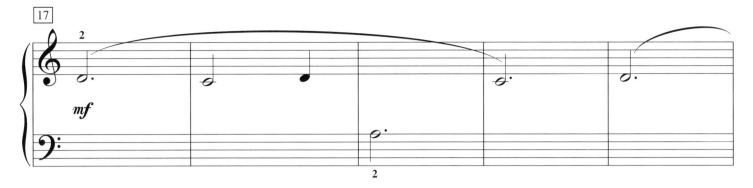

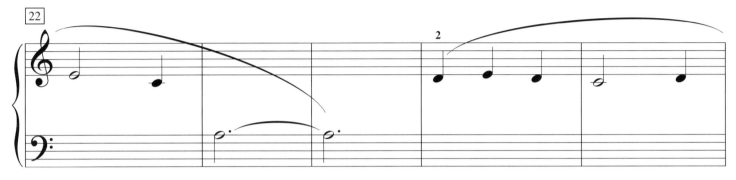

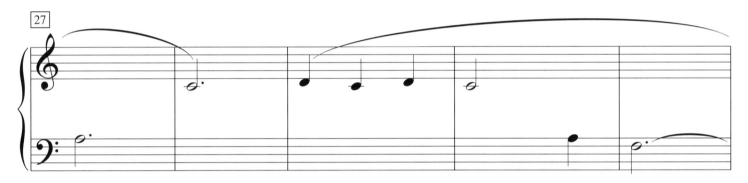

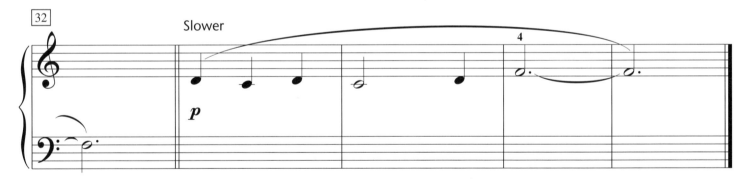

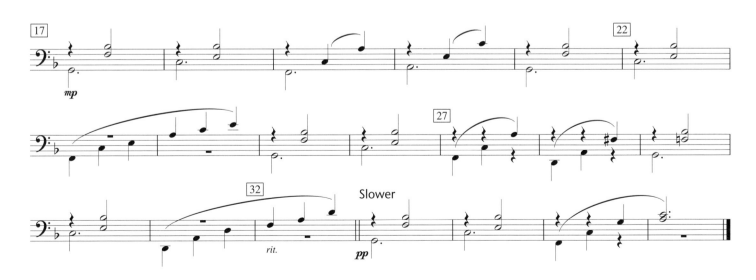

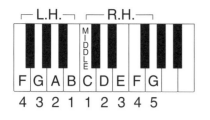

Jazz Jig

Phillip Keveren

With driving energy (♩ = 184)

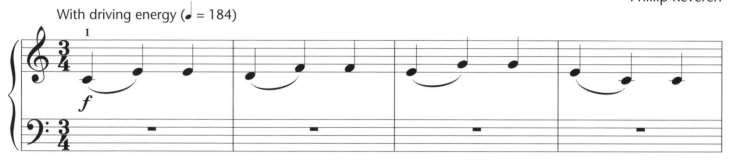

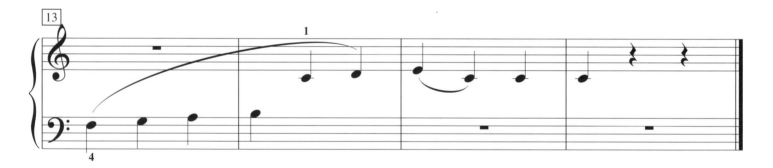

Accompaniment (Student plays one octave higher than written.)

TRACKS 73/74   TRACK 43

With driving energy (♩ = 184)

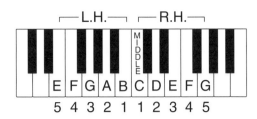

Russian Dance
"Trepak"
from the ballet THE NUTCRACKER

Pyotr Il'yich Tchaikovsky
(1840-1893)
Arranged by Fred Kern

Lively (♩ = 168)

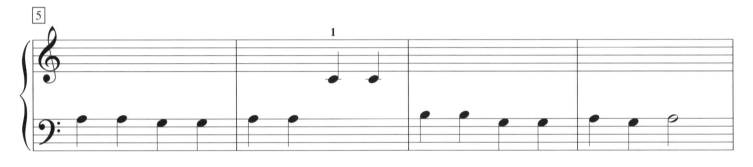

Accompaniment (Student plays one octave higher than written.)

TRACKS 75/76 TRACK 44

Lively (♩ = 168)

WHOLE REST

Whole Rest means to rest for an entire measure.

DYNAMIC SHADING

crescendo   **decrescendo**

gradually louder   gradually softer

Dynamic Shading is created by gradually changing from soft to loud or loud to soft.

Technique Tip   To play *crescendo* or *decrescendo*, press the key to the bottom of the keybed with increasing or decreasing arm weight.

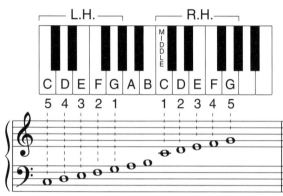

Rope Bridge

Smoothly (♩ = 120)

Accompaniment (Student plays one octave higher than written.)

TRACKS 1/2   TRACK 1

Smoothly (♩ = 120)

C Major Pattern
C-D-E-F-G

Technique Tip | Play the following warm-up. Balance the weight of your arm over each finger as you move smoothly from key to key. Let your arm follow your fingers as you play.

Smoothly ($\quarternote$ = 120) — **TRACKS 3/4** — **TRACK 2**

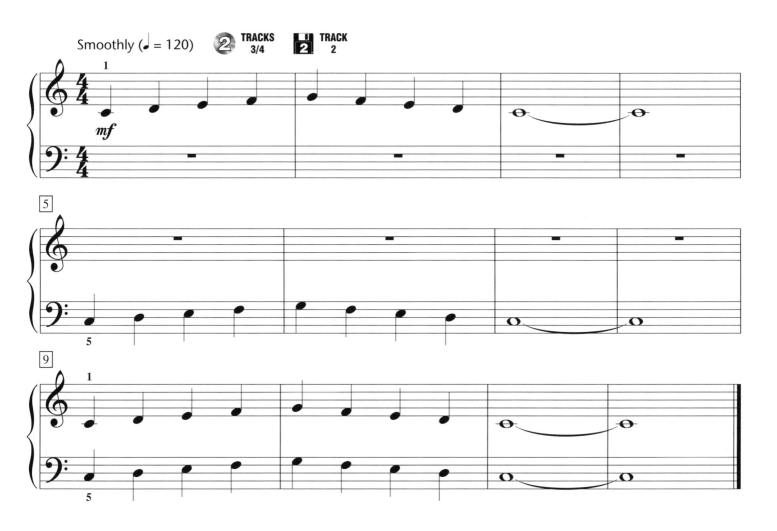

Ad Lib | **An Improvisation**

1. Place both hands on **C-D-E-F-G**. Listen and feel the pulse as your teacher plays the accompaniment below.
2. Experiment by playing **C-D-E-F-G**, first with your right hand, then with your left hand.
3. Improvise with each hand.

Accompaniment
Moderately ($\quarternote$ = 120) — **TRACK 5** — **TRACK 3**

Repeat as necessary | Last time

Song of the Orca

Phillip Keveren

MELODIC and HARMONIC INTERVALS

Melodic Intervals – Notes played consecutively make a melody.
Harmonic Intervals – Notes played together make harmony.

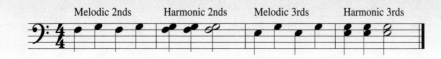

Interval Etude

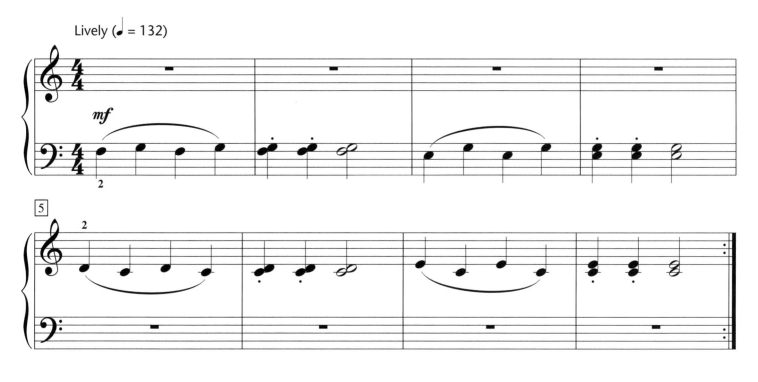

Accompaniment (Student plays two octaves higher than written.)

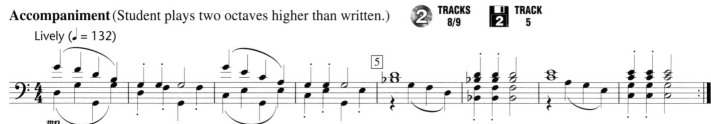

La Cha-Cha

Phillip Keveren

Accompaniment (Student plays one octave higher than written.)

D.C. (Da Capo) al Fine

D.C. (Da Capo) al Fine means to return to the beginning and play to the **Fine** sign.

The form of this piece is **A-B-A**.

FORTISSIMO

$\boldsymbol{ff}$

means play very loudly

INTERVAL of a 4th

On the piano, a 4th
– skips two keys
– skips two fingers
– skips two letters

On the staff, a 4th
– skips two notes
 from either a line
 to a space or a
 space to a line.

Hoedown

Janet Medley

PIANISSIMO

pp

means play very softly

Sunlight Through the Trees

Phillip Keveren

Flowing (♩ = 120)

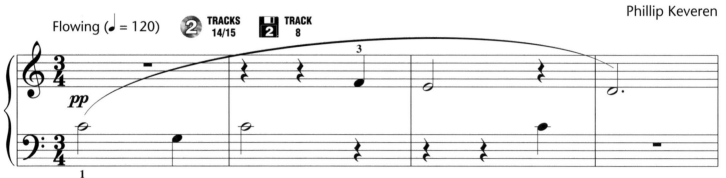

Play one octave higher than written and hold down damper pedal throughout.

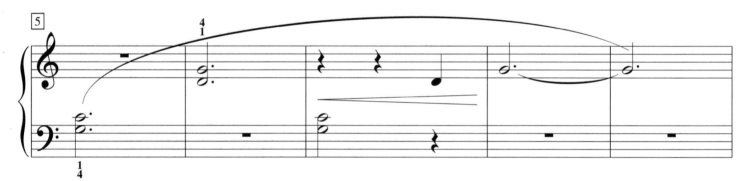

In My Dreams

Jennifer Linn

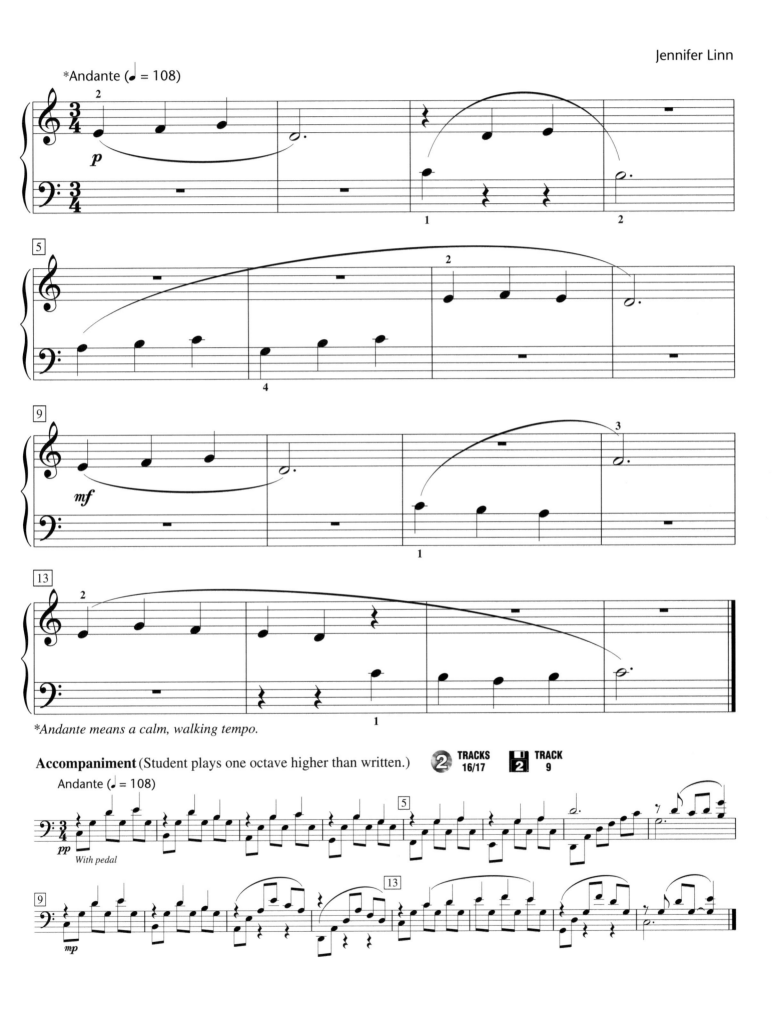

*Andante means a calm, walking tempo.

Accompaniment (Student plays one octave higher than written.)

Directional Reading and Writing

1. Play each series of intervals below.

2. Write the name of the last note in the box.

3. Draw the notes for each exercise on the staff.

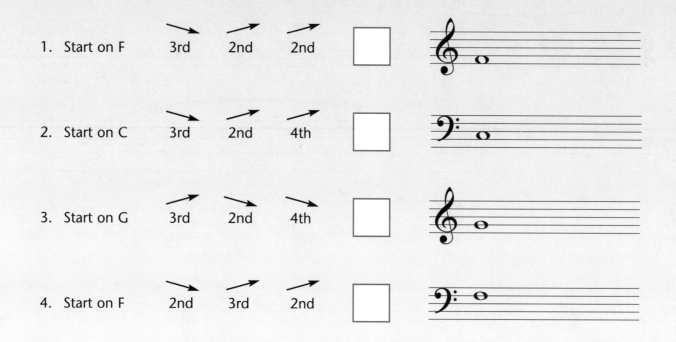

1. Start on F   3rd   2nd   2nd

2. Start on C   3rd   2nd   4th

3. Start on G   3rd   2nd   4th

4. Start on F   2nd   3rd   2nd

Interval Reading and Ear Training

Study each three-note example below.

1. Do the notes move by 2nds, 3rds, or 4ths? Circle the correct answer.

2. Listen as your teacher plays one pattern from each box.
   Circle the pattern that was played.

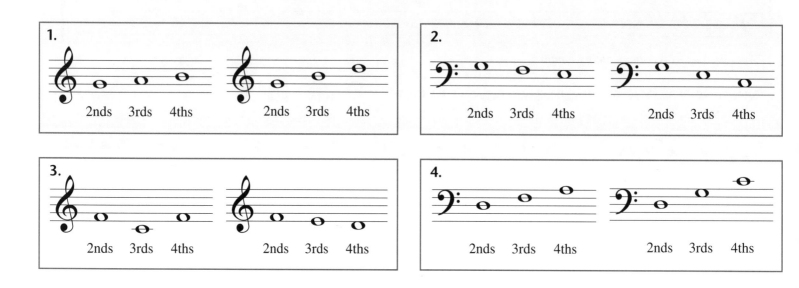

FLAT

♭

A **Flat** sign before a note means to play the next key to the left, whether black or white. When a flat appears before a note, it remains flat for the entire measure.

Too Cool!

Phillip Keveren

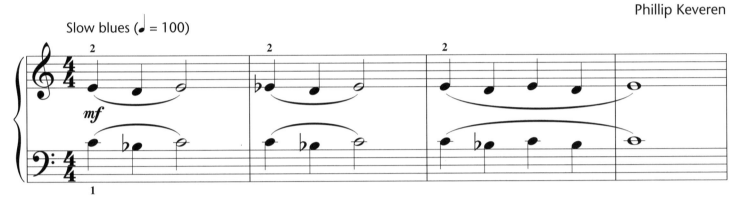

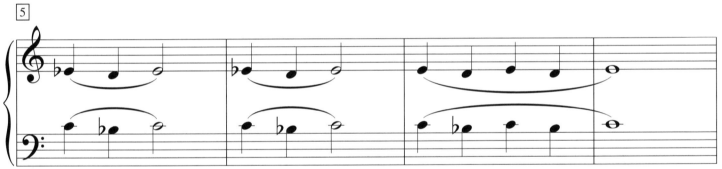

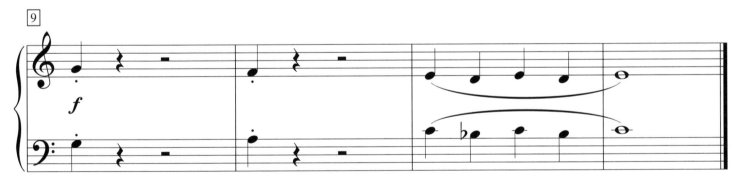

Accompaniment (Student plays one octave higher than written.) ② **TRACKS 18/19** 🎹 **TRACK 2 10**

ACCENT

>

An **Accent** over or under a note
means to play that note louder.

A Little Latin

Bill Boyd

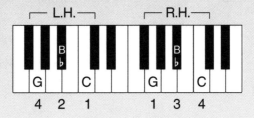

Ad Lib | An Improvisation

Let your hands talk to each other!

1. One way to create an improvised melody is to trade phrases between the hands.
2. As your teacher plays the accompaniment, make up your own melody using the notes shown on the keyboard below.

Accompaniment
Moderately fast (♩ = 84)

TRACK 22

TRACK 12

8va - - - ┐

When the sign *8va - - -┐* appears over a note or a group of notes, play the note or notes one octave (eight notes) higher than written.

15ma - - - ┐

Play two octaves higher than written.

Little Star

Traditional French
Arranged by Phillip Keveren

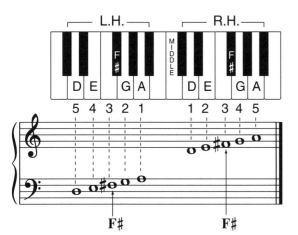

Andantino

Louis Köhler
(1820-1886)
Adapted by Fred Kern

*Andantino (♩ = 132)   TRACKS 25/26   TRACK 14

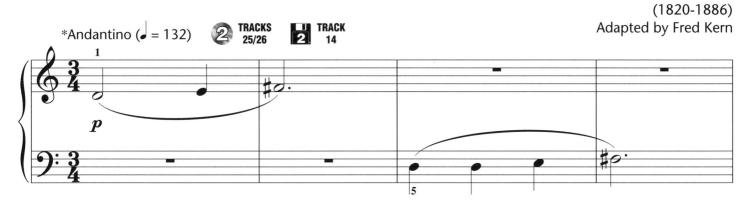

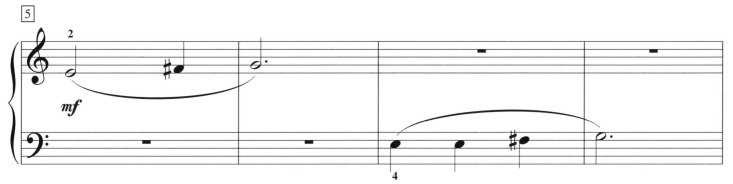

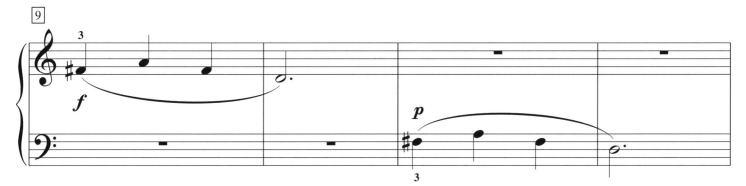

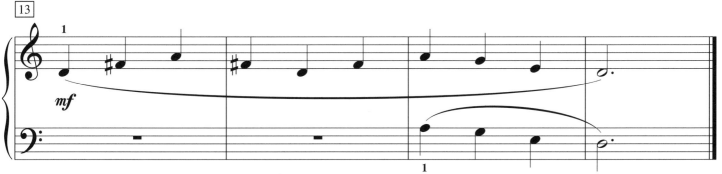

Andantino is a slightly faster tempo than Andante.

Shifting Winds

Phillip Keveren

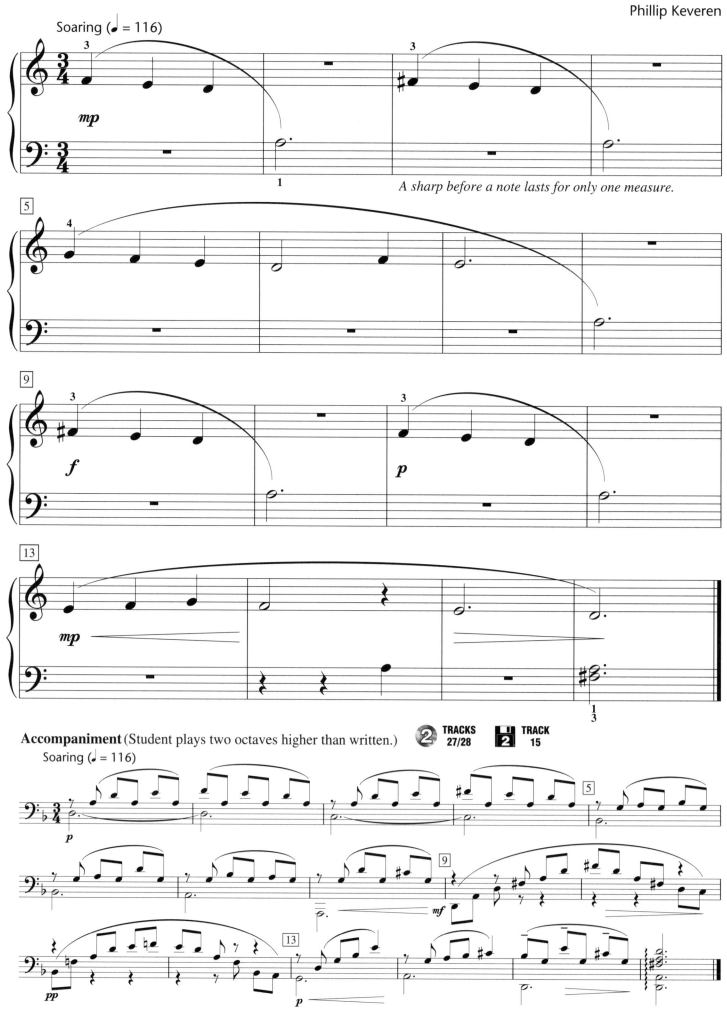

A sharp before a note lasts for only one measure.

Accompaniment (Student plays two octaves higher than written.)

Quiet Thoughts

J.H. Berens, Op. 62
(1826-1880)
Adapted by Fred Kern

Accompaniment (Student plays one octave higher than written.)

TRACKS 29/30   TRACK 16

Peacefully (♩ = 100)

Star Quest

Phillip Keveren

Accompaniment (Student plays one octave higher than written.) TRACKS 31/32 TRACK 17

Heroic march (♩ = 120)

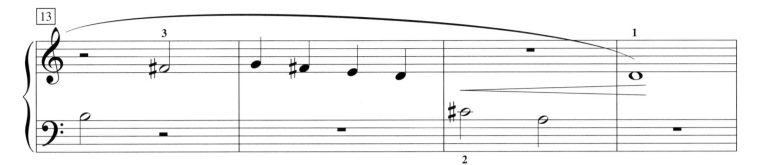

NATURAL	**FERMATA**
A **Natural** sign cancels a sharp or flat. Play the natural (white) key.	A **Fermata** means to hold a note longer than its rhythmic value.

Bayou Blues

Phillip Keveren

Hold down
damper pedal

Release

64

INTERVAL of a 5th

On the piano, a 5th
- skips three keys
- skips three fingers
- skips three letters

On the staff, a 5th
- skips three notes
  from either a line
  to a line or a
  space to a space.

| Technique Tip | Changing Positions |

When moving from one position to another, use your thumb or fifth finger as a guide.
Look ahead. Plan your move to the new position.

Canyon Echoes

Phillip Keveren

Slowly and spaciously (♩ = 112)

TRACKS 35/36   TRACK 19

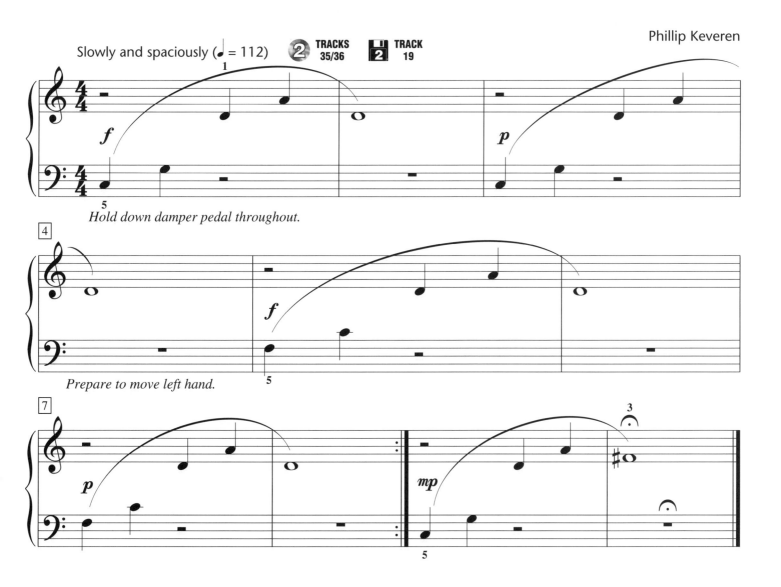

Hold down damper pedal throughout.

Prepare to move left hand.

RITARD

Ritard or **rit.** means to slow the tempo gradually.

Gentle Rain

Phillip Keveren

Slowly and steadily (♩ = 76)
Both hands 8va throughout.

TRACKS
37/38

TRACK
20

EIGHTH NOTES

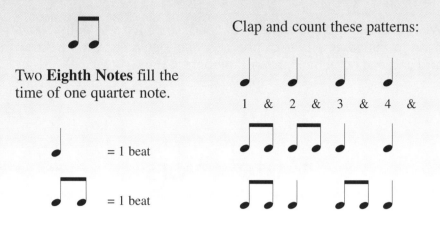

Two **Eighth Notes** fill the time of one quarter note.

♩ = 1 beat

♫ = 1 beat

Clap and count these patterns:

1 & 2 & 3 & 4 &

Little River Flowing

Folk Melody

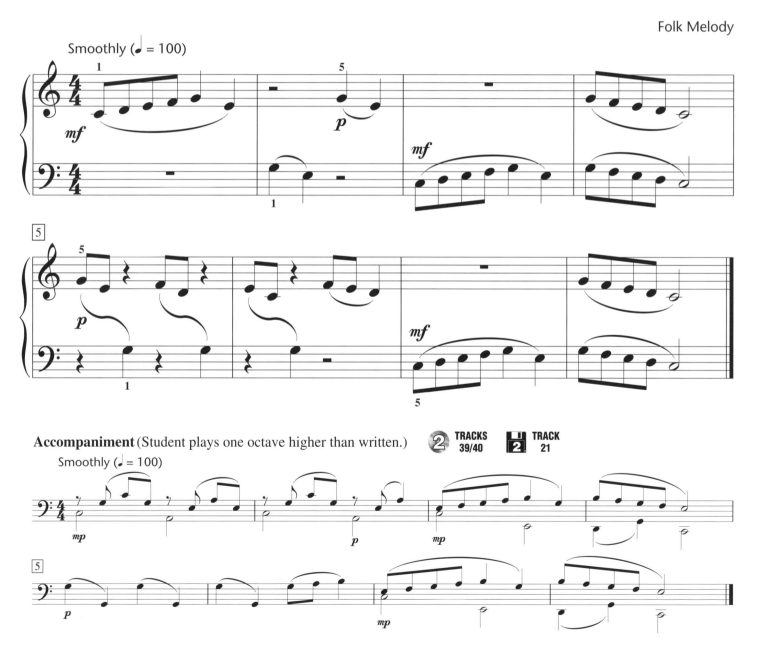

Accompaniment (Student plays one octave higher than written.)

TRACKS 39/40   TRACK 21

Smoothly (♩ = 100)

When playing *legato* from hand to hand, strive for a smooth follow-through from one hand to the other. Play each phrase *legato*, beginning with a downward motion of the arm and ending with an upward motion of the wrist.

Watercolors

Phillip Keveren

Shooting Hoops

Phillip Keveren

UPBEAT (Pick-up)

A note that comes before the first full measure is called an **Upbeat**.

Count: "4   1   2   3   4"

Spring
from THE FOUR SEASONS

Antonio Vivaldi
(1678-1741)
Arranged by Fred Kern

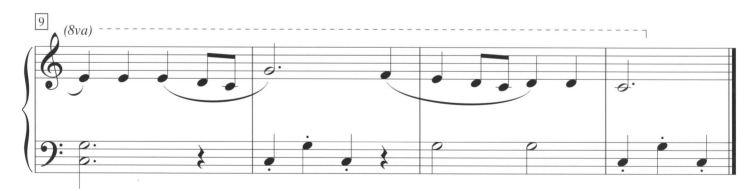

G Major Pattern
G-A-B-C-D

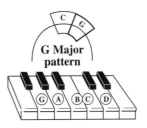

Ad Lib	An Improvisation

Place both hands on **G-A-B-C-D**. As your teacher plays the accompaniment below, improvise a melody using one hand or the other.

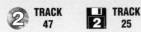

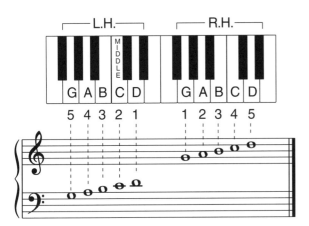

You already know how to play *Shooting Hoops* in the C Major pattern. Now play the piece in the G Major pattern.

Shooting Hoops

Phillip Keveren

G MAJOR WARM-UP

G Major pattern

Alouette

French Folk Melody
Arranged by Phillip Keveren

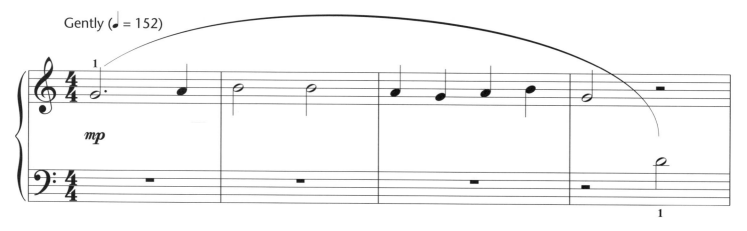

Gently (♩ = 152)

Accompaniment (Student plays one octave higher than written.) TRACKS 48/49 TRACK 26

Gently (♩ = 152)

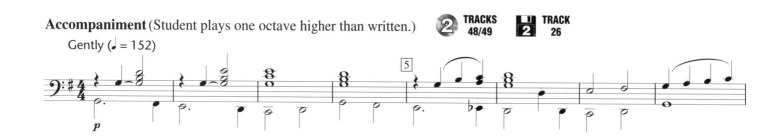

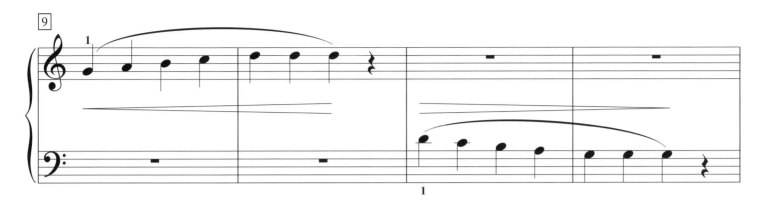

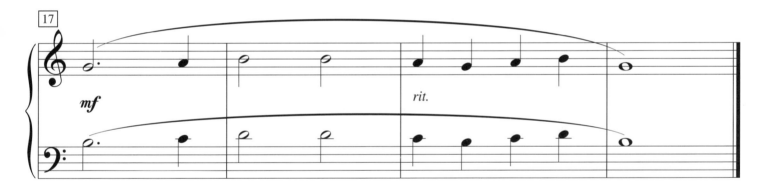

Allegro

Anton Diabelli
(1781-1858)
Adapted by Fred Kern

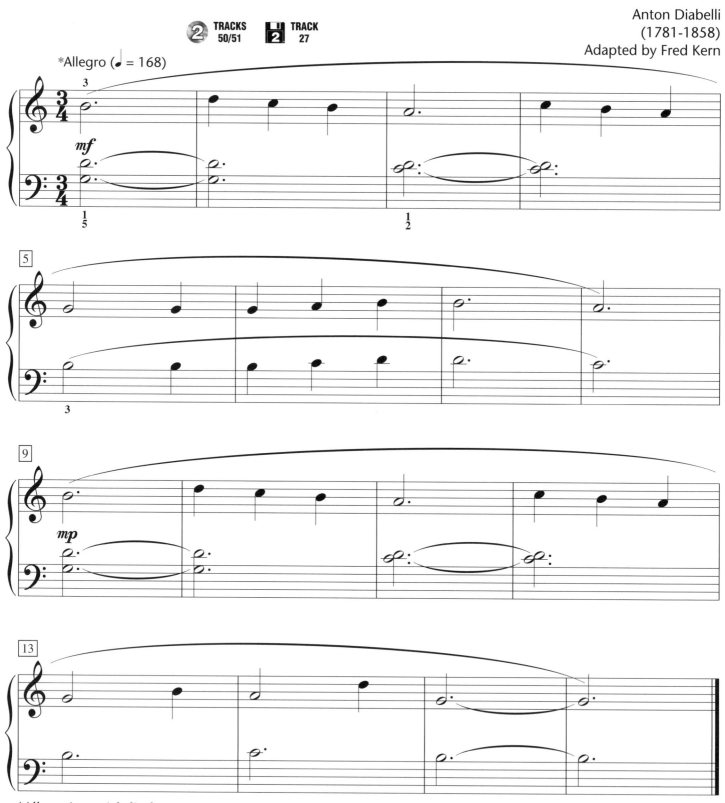

*Allegro is a quick, lively tempo.

Handbells

Fred Kern

Accompaniment (Student plays as written.)

TRACKS 52/53   TRACK 28

Ringing (♩ = 112)

Play both hands 8va throughout.

mf With pedal; sempre legato

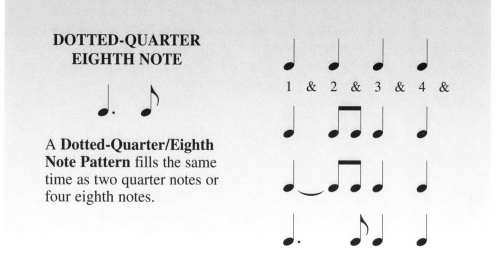

DOTTED-QUARTER EIGHTH NOTE

A **Dotted-Quarter/Eighth Note Pattern** fills the same time as two quarter notes or four eighth notes.

Ode to Joy

Ludwig van Beethoven
(1770-1827)
Arranged by Phillip Keveren

Boogie-Woogie Style for *Boogie Baby*

The boogie-woogie style of piano playing features up-tempo rhythms and a repeated pattern in the bass. The right hand improvises melodic variations over blues harmony.

Listen as your teacher plays the Style Clip below.

Boogie-Woogie Style Clip

Boogie-Woogie Patterns

Parallel harmonic patterns such as these are often used in boogie-woogie style music. Play the left-hand patterns below as preparation for *Boogie Baby* (page 78).

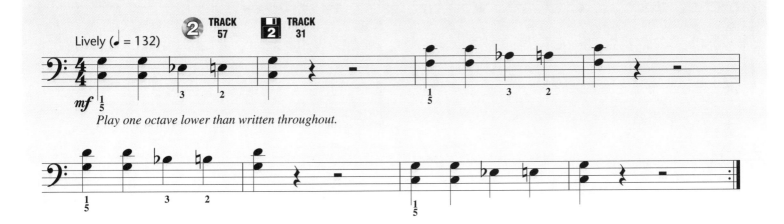

INTERVAL of a 6th

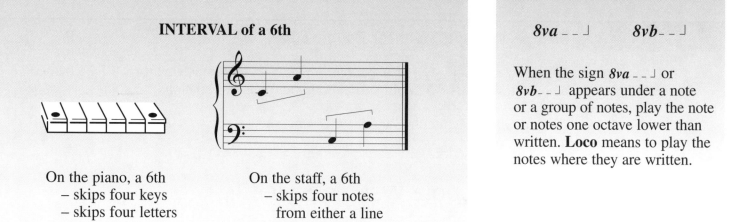

On the piano, a 6th
 – skips four keys
 – skips four letters

On the staff, a 6th
 – skips four notes
   from either a line
   to a space or a
   space to a line.

8va ‒ ‒ ⌐   *8vb* ‒ ‒ ⌐

When the sign *8va* ‒ ‒ ⌐ or
8vb ‒ ‒ ⌐ appears under a note
or a group of notes, play the note
or notes one octave lower than
written. **Loco** means to play the
notes where they are written.

Boogie Baby

Folk Song
Arranged by Mona Rejino

Lavender Mood

Folk Melody
Arranged by Phillip Keveren

Trumpet Tune

Henry Purcell
(1659-1695)
Arranged by Mona Rejino

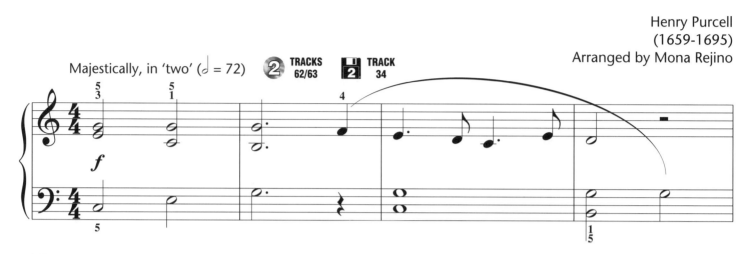

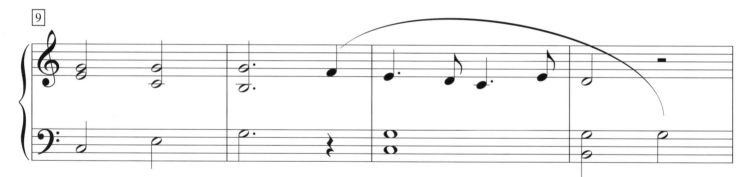

All Through the Night

Traditional Welsh Melody
Arranged by Fred Kern

Serenely (♩ = 76)

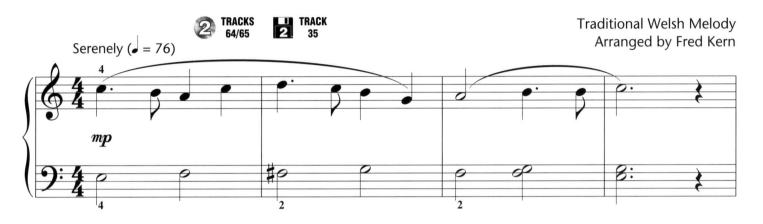

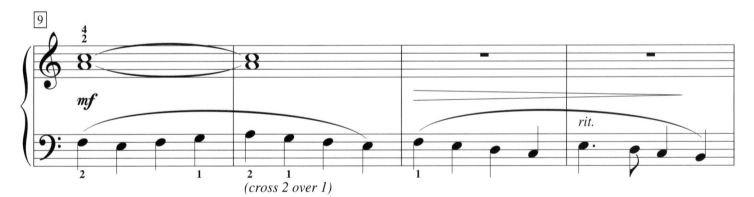

(cross 2 over 1)

* **A tempo** means to return to the original speed.

Viva La Rhumba!

Carol Klose

Accompaniment (Student plays one octave higher than written.)

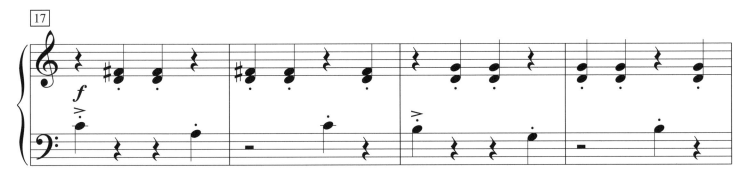

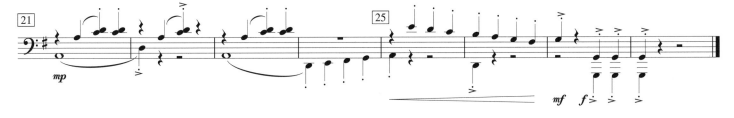

Leap Frog

Carol Klose

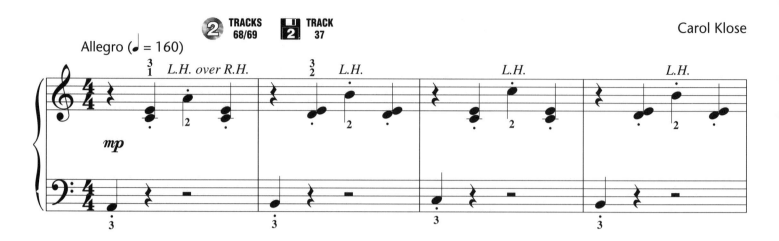

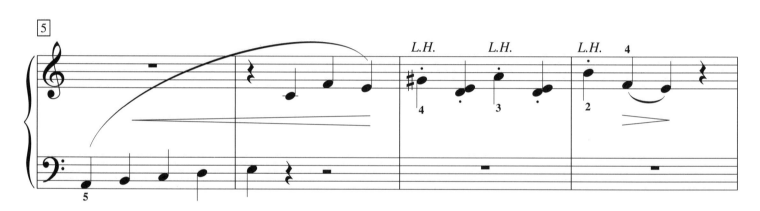

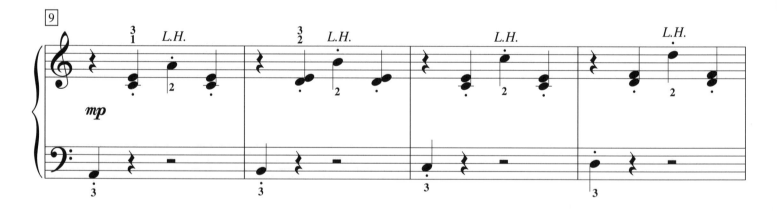

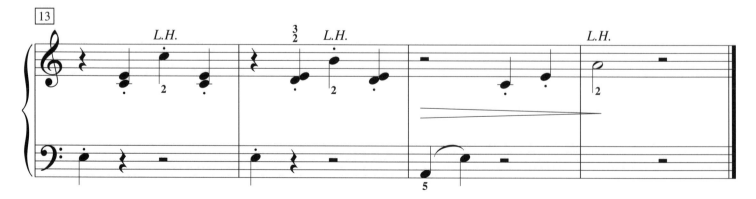

Mirror Image Cs – A Shortcut to Reading Ledger Lines

Notice how the high Cs and the low Cs in the treble and bass clefs mirror each other.

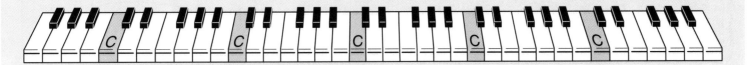

Play all the Cs with your third finger.

A-C-E Groups

Notice the following **A-C-E** groups on the grand staff. Ledger lines are for notes above or below the staff. Locate and play each of the groups on the keyboard.

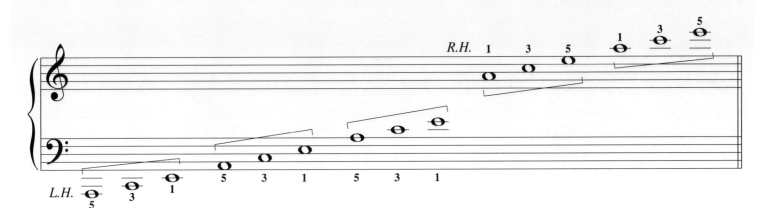

DAMPER PEDAL

The **Damper Pedal** releases the dampers
from the strings, causing the sound to
vibrate longer. Press the pedal down with
your right foot, keeping your heel on the
floor. The symbol below tells you when to
use the pedal.

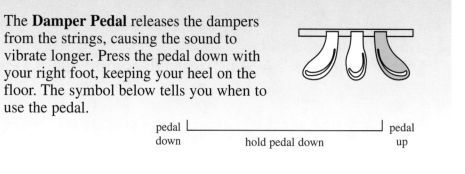

pedal
down   hold pedal down   pedal
up

In Concert

Fred Kern and
Phillip Keveren

86

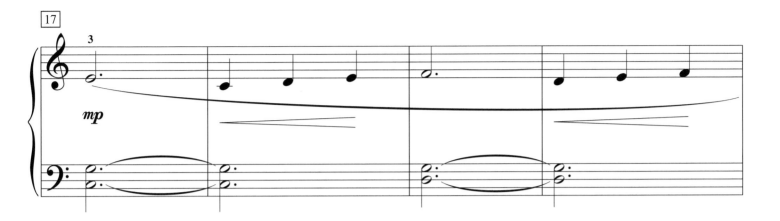

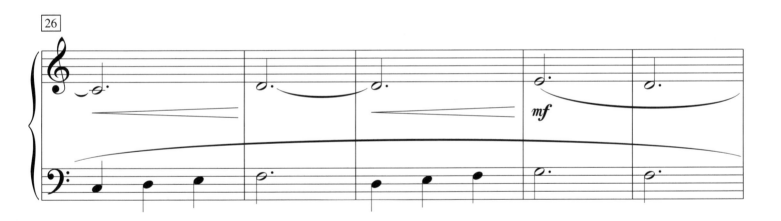

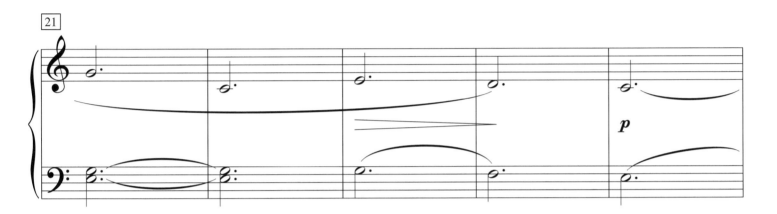

D.C. al Fine

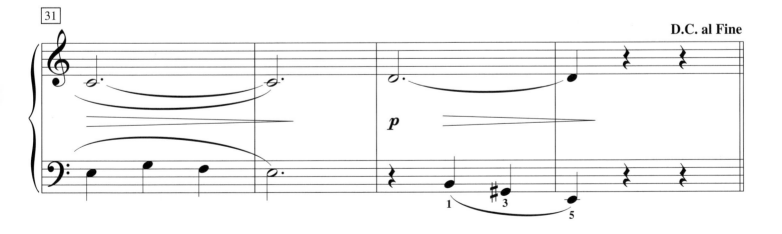

Triads (Chords)

1. A **triad** is a three-note chord that is written on three consecutive lines or three consecutive spaces. The letter name of the chord is the same as the bottom note, the **root**.

Write the letter name of each root in the blank under the chord.

Play each chord in the correct place on the keyboard. Use fingers 1-3-5 in the right hand or 5-3-1 in the left hand.

2. The three notes of a triad (**root-third-fifth**) are tones 1, 3, and 5 of its five-finger pattern.

Name each triad on the keyboard by writing its chord symbol (letter name) in the box.

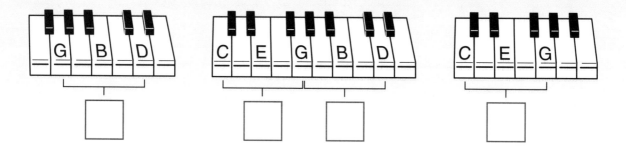

Quick-Lick Parallel chord patterns such as these are often used in popular music. Play the following Quick-Lick using fingers 1-3-5 for each chord in the right hand.

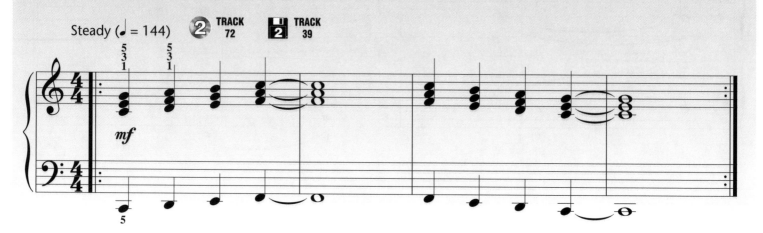

Mystic Mood

Fred Kern and
Brenda Dillon

Accompaniment (Student plays one octave higher than written.)

TRACKS 73/74   TRACK 40

Slowly (♩ = 88)

Rush Hour

Phillip Keveren

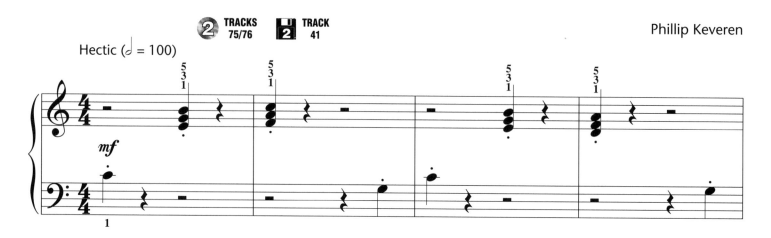

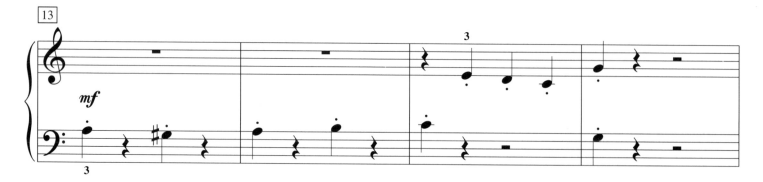

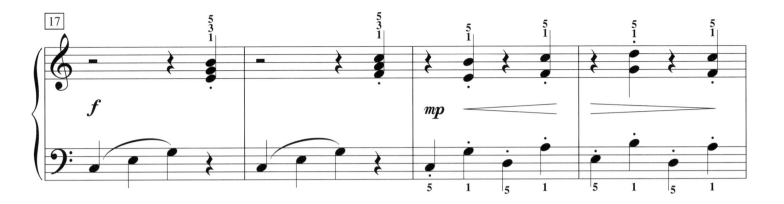

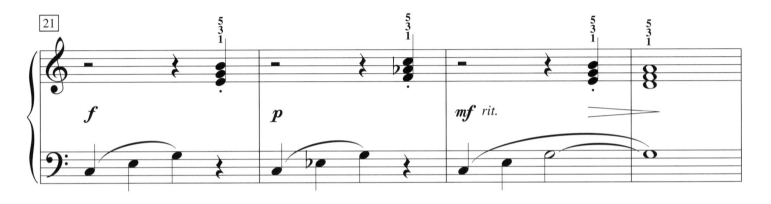

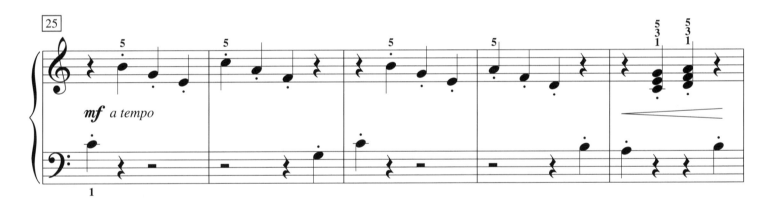

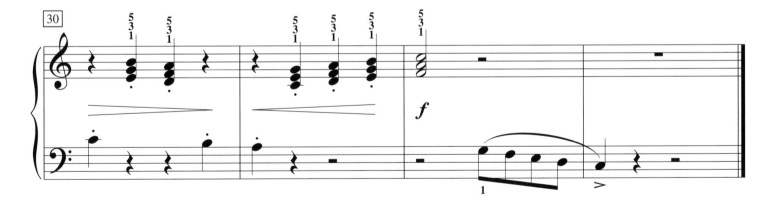

Theme from "The New World" Symphony

Second Movement Theme (Largo)

Antonín Dvořák
(1841-1904)
Arranged by Mona Rejino

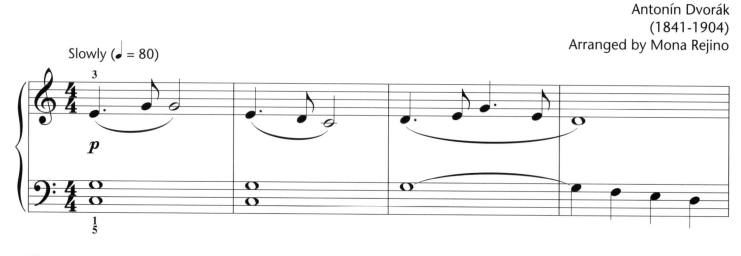

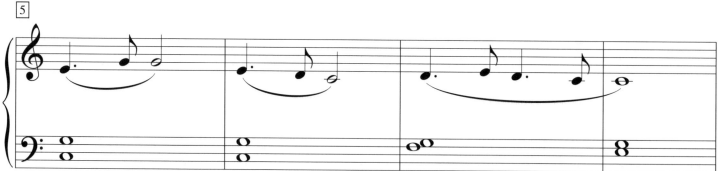

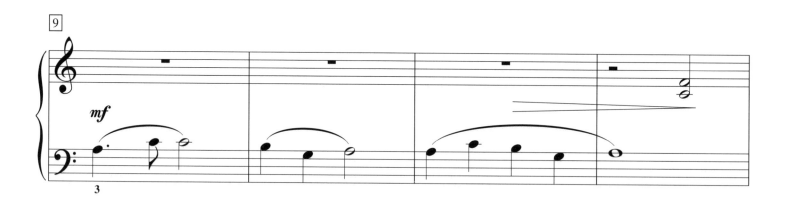

Accompaniment (Student plays one octave higher than written.)

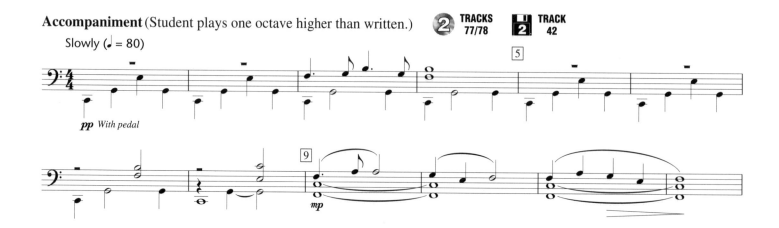

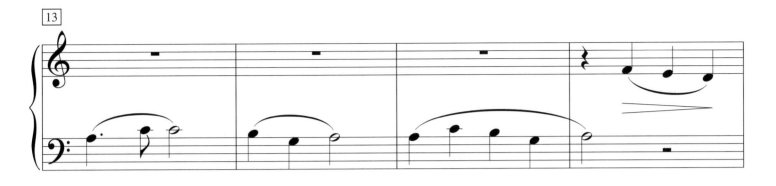

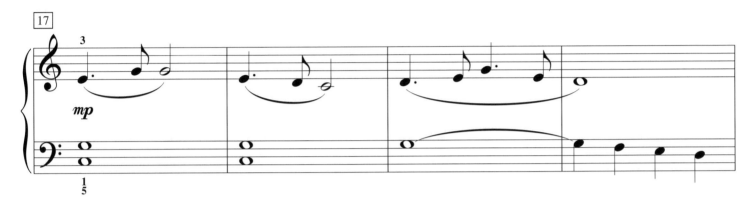

3/4 Time Signature $\frac{3}{4}$	Three beats fill every measure and a quarter note gets one beat.
4/4 Time Signature $\frac{4}{4}$	Four beats fill every measure and a quarter note gets one beat.
8va/8vb/Loco	When the sign *8va* appears over or under a note or a group of notes, play the note or notes one octave (eight notes) higher or lower than written. *8vb* means to play one octave lower. *Loco* means to play the notes where they are written.
15ma	When the sign *15ma* appears over or under a note or group of notes, play the notes two octaves higher or lower than written.
A tempo	*A tempo* means to return to the original speed.
Accent	An **Accent** over or under a note means to play that note louder.
Allegro	**Allegro** means a quick, lively tempo.
Andante	**Andante** means a relaxed, walking tempo.
Andantino	**Andantino** is a slightly faster tempo than **Andante**.
Bass Clef	The notes written in the **Bass Clef** are usually played with the **left hand**.
Crescendo	*Crescendo* means to play gradually louder.
Da Capo al Fine	**D.C. (Da Capo) al Fine** means to return to the beginning and play to the **Fine** sign.
Damper Pedal	The **Damper Pedal** releases the dampers from the strings, causing the sound to vibrate longer. Press the pedal down with your right foot, keeping your heel on the floor.
Decrescendo	*Decrescendo* means to play gradually softer.
Dotted Half Note	A **Dotted Half Note** fills the time of three quarter notes.
Dotted-Quarter/Eighth Note	A **Dotted-Quarter/Eighth Note** pattern fills the same time as two quarter notes or four eighth notes.
Dynamic Shading	**Dynamic Shading** is created by gradually changing from soft to loud or loud to soft.
Eighth Notes	Two **Eighth Notes** fill the time of one quarter note.
Fermata	A **Fermata** means to hold a note longer than its rhythmic value.
Flat ♭	A **Flat** sign before a note means to play the next key to the left, whether black or white. When a **flat** appears before a note, it remains **flat** for the entire measure.
Forte *f*	**Forte** means to play loudly.
Fortissimo *ff*	**Fortissimo** means to play very loudly.
Grand Staff	The **Bass Staff** and the **Treble Staff** together make the **Grand Staff**.
Half Note	A **Half Note** fills the time of two quarter notes.
Half Rest	A **Half Rest** fills the time of two quarter rests.
Harmonic Intervals	**Harmonic Intervals** are notes played together to make harmony.
Interval	An **Interval** is the distance from one note to another.
Interval of a 4th	A **4th** skips two keys on the piano, skips two fingers, and skips two letters. On the staff, a **4th** skips two notes from either a line to a space or a space to a line.

Interval of a 5th	On the piano, a **5th** skips three keys, skips three fingers, and skips three letters. On the staff, a **5th** skips three notes from either a line to a line or a space to a space.
Interval of a 6th	On the piano. A **6th** skips four keys and four letters. On the staff, a **6th** skips four notes from either a line to a space or a space to a line.
Legato	*Legato* indicates smooth and connected playing with no break in the sound.
Lines and Spaces	Notes are written on **Lines** and in **Spaces**.
Measures	Bar lines group beats into **Measures**.
Melodic Intervals	**Melodic Intervals** are notes played consecutively to make a melody.
Mezzo Forte *mf*	**Mezzo Forte** means to play medium loud.
Mezzo Piano *mp*	**Mezzo Piano** means to play medium soft.
Natural ♮	A **Natural** sign cancels a sharp or flat. Play the natural (white) key.
Notes	**Notes** are symbols for sounds. They indicate how long sounds last.
Phrase	A **Phrase** is a musical clause or sentence. Slurs often divide music into phrases.
Piano *p*	**Piano** means to play softly.
Pianissimo *pp*	**Pianissimo** means to play very softly.
Quarter Note ♩	A **Quarter Note** lasts for one pulse (beat).
Quarter Rest 𝄽	A **Quarter Rest** lasts for one pulse (beat).
Repeat Sign :‖	A **Repeat Sign** means play the piece, or sections of the piece, again.
Rests	**Rests** are symbols for silence.
Ritard	*Ritard* or *rit.* means to slow the tempo gradually.
Sharp ♯	A **Sharp** sign before a note means to play the next key to the right, whether black or white. When a **sharp** appears before a note, it remains **sharp** for the entire measure.
Skips (3rds)	On the piano, a **3rd** skips a key, skips a finger and skips a letter. On the staff a **3rd** skips a letter from either line to line or space to space.
Slur	A **Slur** is a curved line over or under a group of notes that means to play smoothly (*legato*).
Staccato	A dot over or under a note means to play the note **Staccato**, or detached.
Steps (2nds)	On the piano, a **2nd** moves from one key to the next. On the staff, a **2nd** moves from a line to a space or a space to a line.
Tie	A **Tie** is a curved line that connects two notes of the same pitch. Hold one sound for the combined value of both notes.
Treble Clef 𝄞	The notes written in the **Treble Clef** are usually played with the **right hand**.
Upbeat (Pick-up)	A note that comes before the first full measure is called an **Upbeat**.
Whole Note 𝅝	A **Whole Note** fills the time of four quarter notes.
Whole Rest ▬	A **Whole Rest** means to rest for an entire measure.

INDEX